Finding God®

Our Response to God's Gifts

As I open this book, I open myself
to God's presence in my life.
When I allow God's grace to help me,
I see with truth, hear with forgiveness,
and act with kindness.
Thank you, God, for your presence in my life.

Barbara F. Campbell, M.Div., D.Min.

James P. Campbell, M.A., D.Min.

LOYOLA PRESS.
A JESUIT MINISTRY
Chicago

IMPRIMATUR	IN CONFORMITY
In accordance with c. 827, permission to publish is granted on May 7, 2019 by Most Reverend Ronald A. Hicks, Vicar General of the Archdiocese of Chicago. Permission to publish is an official declaration of ecclesiastical authority that the material is free from doctrinal and moral error. No legal responsibility is assumed by the grant of this permission.	The Subcommittee on the Catechism, United States Conference of Catholic Bishops, has found this text, copyright 2021, to be in conformity with the *Catechism of the Catholic Church*.

Finding God: Our Response to God's Gifts is an expression of the work of Loyola Press, a ministry of the Society of Jesus, the Jesuits.

Loyola Press has made every effort to locate the copyright holders for the cited works used in this publication and to make full acknowledgment for their use. In the case of any omissions, the publisher will be pleased to make suitable acknowledgments in future editions.

Acknowledgments
Scripture excerpts are from the *New American Bible, Revised Edition*, © 2010, 1991, 1986, 1970 Confraternity of Christian Doctrine, Washington, D.C. All rights reserved. No part of the *New American Bible* may be reproduced in any form without permission in writing from the copyright owner.

Glory Be to the Father, Hail Mary, Lord's Prayer, and Sign of the Cross are from *The Compendium of the Catechism of the Catholic Church* © 2005, Libreria Editrice Vaticana. All rights reserved.

Grace Before Meals, Grace After Meals, and Prayer to One's Guardian Angel are from the *United States Catholic Catechism for Adults* © 2006 United States Conference of Catholic Bishops (USCCB). All rights reserved.

Acknowledgments continue on page 284.

Cover and Interior Design: Loyola Press
Cover Illustration: Marina Seoane

978-0-8294-4624-1

Manufactured in the United States of America.

LOYOLAPRESS.
A JESUIT MINISTRY

www.loyolapress.com
www.findinggod.com

26 27 28 SKY 10 9 8 7 6 5

GRADE 1

Contents

UNIT 1

God, Our Creator and Father

UNIT 1

God, Our Creator and Father

ITALY

Saint Francis of Assisi

Francis liked the country. He loved the trees. He loved the animals. He loved all that God had made.

Once a hungry wolf bothered people. The people were afraid.

Francis was not afraid. He talked to "brother wolf." He gave the wolf some food. Soon, no one was afraid. "Brother wolf" was everyone's friend.

Be Inspired

Praised be You, my Lord, with all Your creatures,
especially Sir Brother Sun
Who is the day and through whom you give
us light.

Saint Francis of Assisi

Be Joyful and Thankful

Saint Francis loved all that God made. He loved the plants. He loved the animals. They made Francis joyful. God's world made him happy. Francis thanked God for all he made.

We can love all that God makes. We can be joyful. We can thank God for all he gives us.

Reading God's Word

It is good to give thanks to the LORD,
to sing praise to your name,
Most High,
To proclaim your love at daybreak,
your faithfulness in the night.

Psalm 92:2–3

ACTIVITY: Give Thanks

Be joyful and thankful. Finish the prayer. Write one thing you thank God for.

Dear God, I thank you for your gift of ______________________

____

____

______________________________.

God Makes Everything

SESSION 1

GOD'S WORD

Read and listen to Genesis 1:1–8.

Paradise, Marina Klett, 2010

God created, or made, the world from nothing. He created everything in the world.

God created the heavens. He created the earth. God created day and night. He created the sky. God created the land and the seas. He created the plants and animals. God created the sun and the moon. He created man and woman.

God looked at his creation. He saw that it was very good. God loves all that he creates. We see God's goodness in his creation.

Prayer

God, help us see the beauty of your creation.
Help us see your goodness.

God Is the Creator

God is the **Creator,** or maker, of everything. He creates everything from nothing. He even creates us.

God creates everything because he loves us. He wants us to enjoy his **creation.** He wants us to love what he creates.

ACTIVITY: God's Creation

Circle things that God creates.

Show Love for God

God loves us. He wants us to be happy. How can we be happy? We can show love for God. We can love one another. We can help others. We can play together. We can care for our world.

Saint Francis of Assisi

We can also show love for God by praying. When we finish, we pray ***Amen.*** This word tells God that we really mean what we said.

Some people show a strong love for God. Francis of Assisi did this. He was a true friend of God. He is a **saint.**

ART PRINT 1

Art Print 1 shows an image of Saint Vincent de Paul helping people in need. What can you do to help others?

Helping Others

Like Saint Vincent de Paul, we can show love for God by helping others. Some people build homes for those in need. Some people share their food and clothes.

ACTIVITY: I Give to Others

Draw a picture of yourself donating items to a St. Vincent de Paul center.

Sign of the Cross

When we pray, we talk to God. We think of him. We begin our prayer with the Sign of the Cross. Then we thank God for all of creation. We ask God for what we need. We tell God we love him. We end our prayer with the Sign of the Cross.

Show God your love. Pray the Sign of the Cross. Then talk to God. End your prayer with the Sign of the Cross and *Amen.*

Prayer

In the name of the Father

and of the Son

and of the Holy

Spirit.

Amen.

God Makes Good Things

God looked at everything he had made, and found it very good.

Genesis 1:31

ACTIVITY: God's World Is Good

Finish the picture. Draw other things that God creates.

Reading God's Word

Let the heavens be glad and the earth rejoice;
  let the sea and what fills it resound;
  let the plains be joyful and all that is in them.
Then let all the trees of the forest rejoice.

Psalm 96:11–12

Living My Faith

Faith Summary

God is the Creator of all people and all things. When we care for others and the world, we show God our love.

Words I Learned

Amen **creation** **Creator** **God** **saint**

Ways of Being Like Jesus

Jesus loves God's creation. *Show that you love God's creation.*

ACTIVITY: Loving God's Creation

Write how you care for God's creation. Finish the sentence.

I care for God's creation.

I care by ______________________

____

______________________________.

Prayer

Thank you, God, for making this beautiful world for us.

With My Family

Scripture Together

God our Father creates all things. By his will and through his works, we see his great power and his great love. We give thanks to God for his goodness.

As a family, read about worshiping God in Revelation 4:11. When you have finished, discuss the Scripture. You may use the following questions to prompt discussion:

- What does God create?
- What do you thank God for?
- How can you show your love for God?

Family Prayer

Pray together:
Thank you, Father, for making us part of your creation. Bless our family and help us care for your world. Amen.

Faith on the Go

Ask one another: *As part of God's creation, how should we use the abilities God gave us?*

ACTIVITY: Care for Creation

As a family, plant seeds in paper cups or in a garden. Tend the plants as they grow, and thank God for his creation. Discuss other ways to care for God's world.

God Cares for Us

SESSION 2

GOD'S WORD

Read and listen to John 3:16–17.

Jesus with children

God the Father cares for us. He loves us. He wants what is best for us. We see his love in the gifts he gives us. We feel his love when we love one another.

God the Father gave us the greatest gift. God sent his Son, Jesus, to us. Jesus shows us how to love. Jesus shows us how to care for others.

When we love and care for others, we grow closer to God the Father. We thank him for his gift. We thank him for his Son, Jesus.

Prayer

Loving God, thank you for the gift of your love. Help us show your love to others.

Showing God We Care

We gather at **Mass** to show God we care. We pray together at Mass. We listen to stories from the Bible. The stories tell us about God's love for us. We sing together. We show our love for God. We receive Holy Communion.

Mass is a special kind of **liturgy.** In a liturgy we pray together. We celebrate the great things God does for us.

Reading God's Word

I believe I shall see the Lord's goodness
in the land of the living.

Psalm 27:13

God gives us wonderful things. At Mass we **praise** God together as one family. We tell God how happy we are for who he is. We thank God for all he does. We use our voices to sing. We show our love for God. We celebrate God's love through prayer.

ACTIVITY: Praise God at Mass

Draw yourself praising God at Mass. Then finish the sentence.

At Mass I praise God by ______________________________.

ART PRINT
2

Art Print 2 shows children helping and showing love for one another. What can you do to show God's love today?

God's Love

God loves us and cares for us. That is why he made us. He made us to be like him. When we love and take care of others, we show our love for God.

ACTIVITY: I Can Show God's Love

Draw a line to complete each sentence correctly. Then read aloud each sentence. Afterward, write about a time you showed God's love.

1. On the playground, I ●
2. When I play a game with someone, I ●
3. When it's time to clean up, I ●
4. If someone is hurt, I ●

● 1. get help for him or her.

● 2. take turns calmly and fairly.

● 3. ask someone to play.

● 4. help put away everyone's things.

____

____

____

____

REFLECT

We Give Thanks

God loves and cares for you and others. You can thank God. You can pray these words.

Prayer

We praise you.
We bless you.
We thank you.

Now, talk with God in your heart. Thank him for the way he cares for you.

God's Perfect World

How do we know God cares for us? He gives us good things. God's world is very good.

> God also said: See, I give you every seed-bearing plant on all the earth and every tree that has seed-bearing fruit on it to be your food.
>
> *Genesis 1:29*

ACTIVITY: God Gives Us Good Things

What good things from God are in the picture? Tell a partner about them. Then color the picture.

Living My Faith

Faith Summary

God loves us. God wants us to love one another. That is why he made us to be like him.

Words I Learned

liturgy **Mass** **praise**

Ways of Being Like Jesus

Jesus cares for others. *Show others you care about them.*

ACTIVITY: God's Love

We can feel God's love. We can show God's love. Finish each sentence.

I feel God's love when ______________________________

____

____.

I show God's love when ______________________________

____

____.

Prayer

Thank you, God, for loving me and showing me how to care for others.

With My Family

Scripture Together

Jesus tells us to love God the Father. Jesus tells us to love our neighbors.

As a family, read about showing love in Mark 12:28–31. When you have finished, discuss the Scripture. You may use the following questions to prompt discussion:

- How must we love God the Father?
- Whom does Jesus tell you to love?
- How can you love your neighbors?

Family Prayer

Pray together:
God our Father, thank you for showing us your love. May we always show your love to one another. Amen.

Faith on the Go

Ask one another: *How do you show love for God?*

ACTIVITY: An Act of Love

How does our family show love for one another? Look through family photographs and make an album of family members showing love for one another.

God Is Our Father

SESSION 3

GOD'S WORD

Read and listen to Matthew 6:9–13.

Amen, Laura James, 2010

God is our loving Father. He watches over us. God wants us to be close to him.

When we pray, we talk to God and listen to him. Prayer helps us grow closer to him. Prayer shows him our love.

What can we say when we pray? We can thank and praise God. We can ask God for help. We can ask for ourselves and others. We thank him for all he gives us. We can also tell him we are sorry. Jesus gives us a prayer. It helps us talk to God, our Father. We call it the Lord's Prayer.

Prayer

Our Father in heaven,
hallowed be your name.

Matthew 6:9

The Word of God

Jesus tells us that God is his Father. He tells us that God is our Father too. We learn this in the **Bible.** The Bible reveals, or tells, the story of God our Father. It tells that our Father loves us. It tells that our Father will care for us. It tells about his Son, Jesus. The Bible is the **Word of God.**

Jesus, the Good Shepherd

ACTIVITY: God's Word

Connect the dots to see the hidden picture.
Then write the word for what you see. Color the picture.

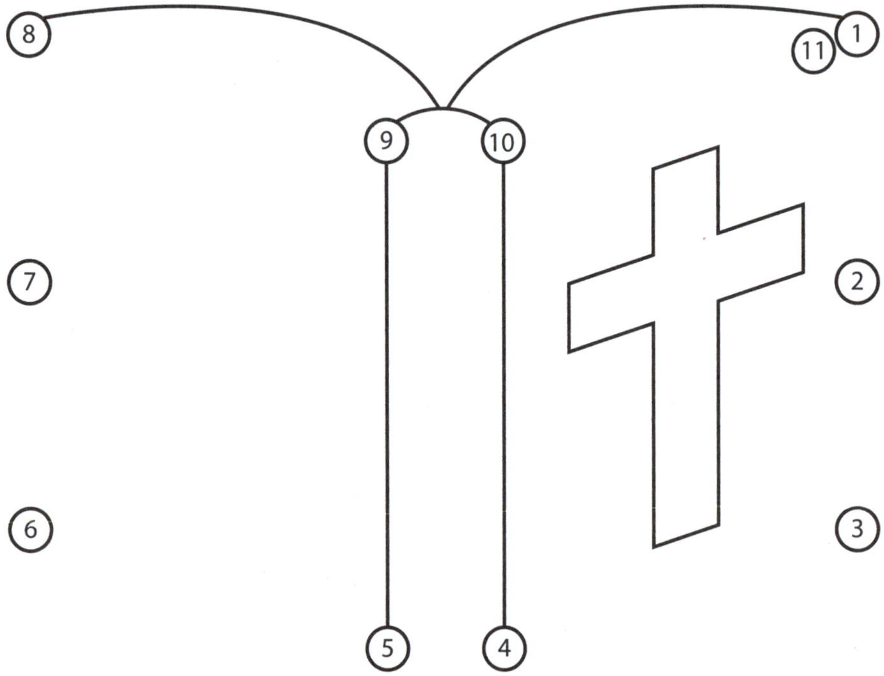

____

Sacred Scripture

The Bible teaches us how God loves and cares for us. We learn what he wants us to do. We learn how to live joyfully.

The Bible is the Word of God. The writings in it are called **Scriptures.** Scriptures are sacred, or holy.

The Old Testament is the first part of the Bible. It tells about God the Father. It tells how the Father always cares for us. The New Testament is the second part. It tells about Jesus. It tells how Jesus lived and what he did. It tells us how we can live joyfully.

Link to Liturgy

At Mass we hear stories from the Bible. We listen to the Word of God.

ART PRINT 3

Art Print 3 shows Jesus on a donkey being welcomed by a large group of children. Where can you learn even more about Jesus?

God Gave Us His Son

God wants us to know about him. God sent his Son, Jesus, to us. Jesus teaches us that God is our Father. He tells us and shows us how much God loves us.

> And a voice came from the heavens, saying, "This is my beloved Son, with whom I am well pleased."
>
> *Matthew 3:17*

ACTIVITY: Jesus Takes Our Hand

On one side of Jesus, draw yourself holding his hand. On the other side, draw a friend or family member holding Jesus' hand.

REFLECT

How Special You Are

Imagine that Jesus is speaking to you. Jesus tells you how special you are! He tells you how much the Father loves you. Now pray the prayer below.

Prayer

Dear Jesus, thank you for being with me. Thank you for hearing me.

Meet Jesus in your heart. Talk to him. Know that he hears your words. Be at peace with Jesus.

At Home with Jesus

Imagine Jesus is coming to your home. How do you greet him? What do you do when Jesus comes?

ACTIVITY: Welcome, Jesus!

Draw Jesus with you and your family in your house. Then write what you will say to him.

Reading God's Word

[Jesus said,] "Whoever loves me will keep my word, and my Father will love him, and we will come to him and make our dwelling with him."

John 14:23

Living My Faith

Faith Summary

We learn about God the Father and his Son, Jesus, in the Bible. Jesus tells us about God's love. Jesus teaches us to pray.

Words I Learned

Bible **Jesus** **Scripture** **Word of God**

Ways of Being Like Jesus

Jesus tells us that God the Father loves us. *Share the Father's love. Say "God loves you." Say "I love you too."*

ACTIVITY: How I Pray

Jesus teaches us how to pray. We can pray anytime and anywhere. The Father always listens. Finish each sentence.

My favorite time to pray is ______________________________

____

____.

My favorite place to pray is ______________________________

____

____.

Prayer

Thank you, Jesus, for teaching us how to pray.

With My Family

Scripture Together

Jesus tells about a father and son. The son makes bad choices, but he is sorry. His father forgives him.

As a family, read about the father and son in Luke 15:11–32. When you have finished, discuss the Scripture. You may use the following questions to prompt discussion:

- Why is the father happy to see his son?
- How do people show you love?
- What do you learn from this story?

Family Prayer

Pray together:
Our Father, help us forgive one another. Amen.

Faith on the Go

Ask one another: *How does God our Father show his love for us?*

ACTIVITY: Family Bible

Read your family Bible together. You might read and discuss Scriptures about forgiveness, such as the parable of the lost sheep in Luke 15:3–7 or the verses about overlooking offenses in Proverbs 10:12, 15:1, and 19:11.

God Gives Us Peace

SESSION 4

GOD'S WORD

Read and listen to John 14:26–27.

The Ascension of Jesus Christ

God the Father loves and welcomes all people. He wants us to live in peace. He sent his Son, Jesus, to bring us his love.

After rising from the dead, Jesus knew his friends were upset. He gave them a gift of peace. He gave them the Holy Spirit. The Holy Spirit guides us to welcome and love everyone. The Holy Spirit brings us the peace of God the Father.

We share God's peace at Mass. We offer one another a Sign of Peace. We can do this with a handshake or by bowing our head. Then we take God's peace with us. We share it with others in the world.

Prayer

Dear God, help me live in peace and share your peace with others.

A Gift of Peace

We learn this Bible story in the Gospel according to John. Jesus' friends were together. They were upset. Jesus came to see them. He wanted to give them peace. He wanted them to share peace with others. Jesus breathed on his friends. He gave them the gift of the **Holy Spirit.**

Jesus gives us the Holy Spirit. The Holy Spirit is always with us. He fills us with God the Father's life. He brings us God's peace.

All Are One

The Father, the Son, and the Holy Spirit are the Holy **Trinity.** They are one God in Three Persons. God reveals himself to us through the Holy Trinity.

God the Father made us out of love. Love and peace are God's gifts to us.

ART PRINT 4

Art Print 4 shows four figures holding up a dove, a symbol for peace. What can you do to bring peace?

Bring Peace

You can bring peace to the world in many ways. You can pray for peace. You can even smile for peace. When you smile, others feel happy and peaceful. They smile too. They pass on the smiles. Soon, everyone is smiling. Peace can be everywhere!

ACTIVITY: "Peace Be with You!"

Draw your smiling face. Add hair.

Color your picture.

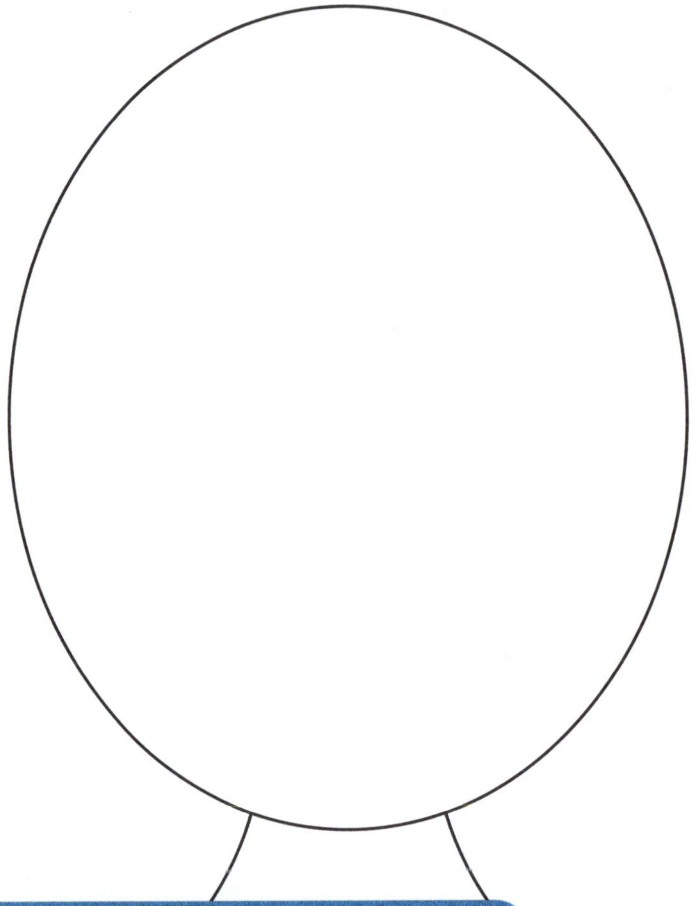

Reading God's Word

Peace be to the brothers, and love with faith, from God the Father and the Lord Jesus Christ. *Ephesians 6:23*

Give Praise

God the Father, God the Son, and God the Holy Spirit are always with us. Talk with them in your heart. Tell them how you will share peace with others.

Prayer

Glory Be to the Father

Glory be to the Father
and to the Son
and to the Holy Spirit,
as it was in the beginning
is now, and ever shall be
world without end.

Father, Son, and Holy Spirit

The Father, the Son, and the Holy Spirit are Three Persons in one God.

ACTIVITY: Three Persons

What do we call the Father, the Son, and the Holy Spirit? Color the spaces that have dots green. Color the other spaces different colors. Then read the words.

Did You Know?

When you see a friend, what do you say? When Saint Francis saw a friend, he said, "Peace and all things good." Try it!

Living My Faith

Faith Summary

God is always with us. God our Father made us. Jesus, his Son, brings us God's love. The Holy Spirit brings us God's peace.

Words I Learned

Holy Spirit **Trinity**

Ways of Being Like Jesus

Jesus brings us the Father's love. *You can bring God's love. Donate your used, unbroken toys to a charity.*

Prayer

Thank you, Holy Spirit, for bringing peace to my life.

ACTIVITY: God's Peace

Draw a picture of you sharing the gift of God's peace. Write what you say when you share God's peace.

"________________________ be with you!"

With My Family

Scripture Together

The Book of Psalms is in the Bible. A psalm is a prayer written like a poem. The psalms are prayers of joy, sorrow, thanksgiving, asking, and praise.

As a family, read the prayer in Psalm 85:9–14. Then discuss the Scripture. You may use the following questions to prompt discussion:

- What does the psalm poet pray will come from God?
- What gifts come to you from God?
- How can you help our family share God's gift of peace?

Family Prayer

Pray together:
Dear God, help us share your peace with one another. Amen.

Faith on the Go

Ask one another: *How can you live in peace with the people around you?*

ACTIVITY: Loving One Another

Take turns talking about times when you sowed peace or could sow peace within the family. You might perform a skit about one of those opportunities for peace.

Celebrating Ordinary Time

SESSION 5

GOD'S WORD

Read and listen to Psalm 104:13–18.

Harvest Time, George Vicat Cole, 1883

Psalms are songs and poems of prayer. Psalms come from a book in the Old Testament of the Bible. At Mass we pray psalms during the Liturgy of the Word. Sometimes we sing a psalm. Other times we say a psalm together.

Psalms are one way we talk with God. Some psalms praise or thank God. They tell God how much we love him. We can praise God for his gifts of creation.

God the Father gives us all we need to live and grow. We thank God for his many gifts.

Prayer

Our Father, thank you for your love and the many gifts you give us.

We Show Thanks During Ordinary Time

We call a year in the Church a **liturgical year.** We use a calendar for the year. The calendar shows important times in the lives of Jesus, Mary, and the saints. It also shows the seasons of the Church. Christmas and Easter are seasons. **Ordinary Time** is the longest season.

During Ordinary Time, we **celebrate,** or praise and worship God. We celebrate from Christmas until Lent. Then we celebrate again from Easter until Advent. We thank God the Father for his many gifts. We show our love for his Son, Jesus, and for one another. During Ordinary Time, we grow closer to God.

Reading God's Word

Give thanks to the LORD, who
is good,
whose love endures forever.

1 Chronicles 16:34

ACTIVITY: Thank you, God!

What do you thank God for? Complete the thank-you card.

Dear God, thank you for ______________________

____

____.

Mass During Ordinary Time

We go to Mass during Ordinary Time. We celebrate God's creation. We thank God for all he creates. We thank God by caring for his creation.

What We Experience

We see flowers or plants around the altar. We see the gifts of bread and wine too. The priest offers the bread and wine at every Mass. These two gifts become Jesus himself. Jesus helps us grow closer to God the Father.

Did You Know?

The liturgical color for Ordinary Time is green.

ACTIVITY: God's Gifts at Mass

Circle the two gifts that the priest offers at every Mass.

ART PRINT
5

Art Print 5 shows a seedling sprouting from the ground. What can you do to give thanks for God's gifts?

Celebrating Ordinary Time

Joyful events happen every day of the year. Each morning we wake up to God's love. The sun rises, and plants grow. Members of God's family are thankful for God's creation and for our many gifts. We celebrate everyday miracles during Ordinary Time. We grow closer to God.

ACTIVITY: My Gift from God

Draw a picture of a joyful event that happened to you today. Then write a sentence about it.

Living My Faith

Faith Summary

Ordinary Time is a time to thank God for all his gifts.

Words I Learned

celebrate
Ordinary Time
liturgical year

Ways of Being Like Jesus

Jesus loves God's creation. *Praise God for the gift of his creation.*

Prayer

Our Father, we praise you and thank you for your gifts!

ACTIVITY: God's Peace

Some psalms thank God for his many gifts. What are you thankful for? Think of things that begin with the letters in *PSALM*. Write your words on the lines.

I am thankful for

P ____________________

S ____________________

A ____________________

L ____________________

M ____________________

AT HOME

With My Family

Scripture Together

Jesus wants us to come to him. He wants us to love his Father. Jesus welcomes all who come to him.

As a family, read Mark 10:13–14. When you have finished, discuss the Scripture. You may use the following questions to prompt discussion:

- Why was Jesus upset?
- How do you greet Jesus each day?
- How can you welcome others as Jesus did?

Family Prayer

Pray together:
Dear Jesus, help us grow in faith together. Amen.

Faith on the Go

Ask one another: *Whom do you pray for today and every day?*

ACTIVITY: Prayer Jar

Make a prayer jar to hold your family's special prayers. Write your prayers on pieces of paper and put them in the jar.

UNIT 2

Jesus, Our Lord and Savior

UNIT 2

Jesus, Our Lord and Savior

ISRAEL

Saint Joseph

Joseph was a carpenter. He made things from wood. He worked hard. Joseph was a good, kind man.

Joseph knew that Mary was going to have a baby. God sent Joseph a message in a dream. God wanted Joseph to marry Mary. God wanted the baby's name to be Jesus. The name *Jesus* means "God saves." Jesus would save God's people.

Joseph became Jesus' father on earth. He cared for Jesus and Mary for the rest of his life.

Be Inspired

Joseph, son of David, do not be afraid to take Mary your wife into your home.

Matthew 1:20

Trust in God

Reading God's Word

May your mercy, LORD, be upon us;
as we put our hope in you.

Psalm 33:22

Joseph listened to God. Joseph did not understand God's plan for him. He trusted God though. He did what God asked. He cared for Mary and Jesus.

We can listen to God too. We may not understand his plan for us. We can trust God though. We can show God our love. We can do what he asks. We can be kind and caring to others.

ACTIVITY: Helping Others

Finish the sentence. Write whom you can help. Write how you can help. Then draw a picture of yourself with that person.

I can help ______________________ by ________________________________ .

God the Father Sends Jesus

SESSION 6

GOD'S WORD

Read and listen to Philippians 2:5–11.

The Holy Family at Nativity,
Laura James, 2007

Our names are important to us. People who know and love us call us by name. We read about Jesus' name in the Bible. His name is holy. It is holy because it came from God the Father.

Jesus is the Son of God. God the Father sent Jesus to us. He sent Jesus to teach us how to love. Jesus died on the Cross for us. He died to save us.

We show respect for Jesus' holy name. We bow our heads. We say Jesus' name with respect. We honor Jesus' name in our prayers.

Prayer

God the Father, help me welcome your Son, Jesus, into my heart.

EXPLORE

Jesus Is Born

In the Gospel of Luke, we learn that **Mary** was going to have a baby. She and **Joseph** were far from home. They had no place to sleep for the night. Imagine how they felt.

Mary and Joseph stayed in a stable. This is where Jesus, the Son of God, was born.

It was a joyous time when Jesus was born. Shepherds were in the fields. God sent his messengers, the **angels,** to the shepherds. The angels sang songs. They told the shepherds where to find Jesus.

Did You Know?

The name *Jesus* means "God saves." Jesus is our Savior.

The Holy Family

God sent his only Son, Jesus, to us. Joseph and Mary cared for him. We call Jesus, Mary, and Joseph the **Holy Family.**

They were a happy family. They loved one another. They learned from one another. Mary and Joseph took care of Jesus. They taught him about God. Jesus obeyed Mary and Joseph.

ACTIVITY: My Family Loves Me

Circle each activity you have learned from your family.

ART PRINT 6

Art Print 6 shows Jesus in a manger surrounded by Mary, Joseph, and shepherds. What comes to mind when you think of the Nativity?

Born in a Stable

Jesus is the Son of God, who became man. He was born in a stable, a shelter for animals such as sheep. Why? God wants to teach us something. He wants us to know that we can find Jesus in unexpected places.

Shepherds were the first to see Jesus. They were everyday people with regular jobs. God wants us to know that Jesus came for all people.

ACTIVITY: Jesus Is Born

Color the Nativity scene.

Reading God's Word

Then the shepherds returned, glorifying and praising God for all they had heard and seen.

Luke 2:20

Prayer to the Holy Family

Think about how Mary and Joseph felt when Jesus was born. Think about this Holy Family. Then open your heart and mind to pray and reflect on the prayer below.

Prayer

Imagine you are with the Holy Family. You are in the stable where Jesus was born. Look around. Whom do you see? What are they doing? Baby Jesus sees you. He reaches out to you.

Jesus is in your arms. You hold him against your heart. Tell Jesus how much you love him.

Now, give baby Jesus back to Mary and Joseph. What do you want to say to the Holy Family?

Jesus, Mary, and Joseph, bless me. Help me follow your example. Help me love others and live together with them in peace.

Who's Who

Think about the Holy Family. Mary was a kind and loving mother. Joseph was a caring father to Jesus on earth. Jesus, the Son of God, grew up as their child.

ACTIVITY: The Holy Family

Look at the pictures below. Write the name of each person on the line. Copy the names from the word box.

Jesus	**Mary**	**Joseph**

____

____

____

Living My Faith

Faith Summary

God showed us his love. He sent us his Son, Jesus. Joseph and Mary were Jesus' parents on earth. Jesus needed them both.

Words I Learned

angel **Holy Family** **Joseph** **Mary**

Ways of Being Like Jesus

Jesus loved Mary and Joseph.
Tell your parents you love them.

Prayer

Thank you, God our Father, for sending your Son, Jesus, to us.

ACTIVITY: Names to Know

Who is in the Holy Family? Read the names in the word box on page 52. Then find and circle the names below.

		Y	J				R	L		
	S	R	O	K		M	A	R	Y	
X	H	Z	S	P	C	N	D	U	N	X
G	Q	J	E	R	R	B	A	A	B	J
P	C	E	P	K	J	E	S	U	S	I
	Q	L	H	Z	J	L	V	R	B	
		D	G	W	Y	G	N	V		
			N	J	Y	L	D			
				T	X	W				
					P					

With My Family

Scripture Together

God sent his Son, Jesus, to us. Through Jesus, we are God's children. God's kingdom can be ours.

As a family, read how Jesus makes us children of God in Galatians 4:4–7. When you have finished, discuss the Scripture. You may use the following questions to prompt discussion:

- What is Jesus' spirit crying out in our hearts?
- What does it mean for you to be a child of God?
- How do you show our family and others that you are God's child?

Family Prayer

Pray together:
Dear God, thank you for the gift of family. Amen.

Faith on the Go

Ask one another: *What one question would you like to ask Mary?*

ACTIVITY: Family Movie Night

Watch a movie about a family. Discuss how the movie shows the family as children of God, loving and helping one another.

Jesus Teaches Us

SESSION 7

GOD'S WORD

Read and listen to Matthew 5:1–12.

Many people followed Jesus. They came to hear him teach. Jesus taught them through words and actions. He told and showed them how to live. He taught them how to love God. He taught them how to pray.

Great crowds followed Jesus as he preached the Good News, Elizabeth Wang, 2004

The Beatitudes are one of Jesus' most important lessons. They teach us how to behave. They give us ways to live as followers of Jesus.

The Beatitudes teach us about choices. They tell and show us how to love God above all things. They teach us how to grow closer to God.

Prayer

Caring Jesus, teach me to love God and others.

EXPLORE

Jesus Prayed to God the Father

Jesus prayed. He talked to God the Father. He listened to God the Father. When we pray a **prayer,** we talk to God the Father. We listen to him in our hearts.

Jesus gave us the Lord's Prayer. When we pray it, we grow closer to God the Father. We grow closer to his Son, Jesus. We grow closer to one another.

Reading God's Word

[Jesus] departed to the mountain to pray, and he spent the night in prayer to God.

Luke 6:12

The Lord's Prayer

The Lord's Prayer is very important. Listen for it at Mass. It starts like this.

Our Father who art in ***heaven,*** →	Our Father is God. Heaven is the life with God that is full of happiness and never ends.
hallowed be thy name; →	God's name is holy.
thy kingdom come, →	We spread the Good News of God's kingdom everywhere on earth.
thy will be done →	We ask God to guide us.
on earth, as it is in heaven. →	We pray that people will do what is pleasing to God.

ART PRINT 7

Art Print 7 shows a woman and child picking cherries in an orchard. How can you serve the Kingdom of God?

Serving the Kingdom

The **Kingdom of God** is God's rule over us. Everyone belongs to the Kingdom of God. Jesus teaches us how to serve the kingdom. We can serve the kingdom in many ways.

ACTIVITY: I Can Serve God's Kingdom

Read each sentence about how you can serve the Kingdom of God. Then draw a picture for each sentence.

Pray for those in need.	Help with a chore at home.
Listen to your teacher.	Be kind to animals.

Did You Know?

Long ago, grown-ups gave pretzels to children who learned their prayers by heart. Why do you think so?

Pray to Jesus

Prepare yourself for praying the first part of the Lord's Prayer. Pray the Sign of the Cross. Then pray the words below.

Prayer

Lord's Prayer

Our Father who art in heaven,
hallowed be thy name;
thy kingdom come,
thy will be done
on earth, as it is in heaven.

Talk to Jesus in your heart. Thank him for teaching you how to pray. Tell Jesus you will talk with God the Father. Tell Jesus you will listen to God the Father as he did.

Serving God's Kingdom

Jesus teaches us about the Kingdom of God. God created the kingdom. We live in God's kingdom in part now on earth. We will live in the kingdom fully in heaven.

God rules the kingdom. He calls us to serve his kingdom. The **Beatitudes** teach us how to serve the Kingdom of God. We serve the kingdom when we do good things.

ACTIVITY: Doing Good Things

Put an X by the picture if someone is serving God's kingdom.

Living My Faith

Faith Summary

Jesus taught us the Lord's Prayer.
It is our most important prayer.

Words I Learned

Beatitudes **Kingdom of God**

heaven **prayer**

Ways of Being Like Jesus

Jesus taught his friends how to pray.
Ask Jesus to help you pray.

Prayer

Thank you, Jesus, for teaching me how to pray and showing me how to love.
I will talk to God every day.

ACTIVITY: Following Jesus' Teachings

We follow Jesus' teachings. The Beatitudes tell us how to serve the Kingdom of God. The Lord's Prayer teaches us how to pray. Read each hint below. Then write the missing letters.

Hint: This teaches us how to pray.

T____e ____or____'s P____a____e____

Hint: These tell us how to serve God's kingdom.

Th____ B____a____it____ ____e____

With My Family

Scripture Together

Before he died, Jesus taught his friends how to treat one another. Jesus told them no one is greater than anyone else. God blesses us as we serve others.

As a family, read about the washing of the feet in John 13:12–17. When you have finished, discuss the Scripture. You may use the following questions to prompt discussion:

- Why did Jesus wash his friends' feet?
- What do you think Jesus is telling us about how we are to relate to one another?
- How can you "wash" the feet of your family members this week?

Family Prayer

Pray together:
Dear God, thank you for teaching us how to live and pray. Amen.

Faith on the Go

Ask one another: *What part of the Lord's Prayer means the most to you?*

ACTIVITY: Family Foot Washing

Have a family foot washing in which family members take turns washing one another's feet. Discuss how no one in the family is more important than the others. Talk about how Jesus calls us to treat one another with love and respect and to serve one another. Discuss how it is equally important to receive love and be grateful when others serve us.

Trust in God

SESSION 8

GOD'S WORD

Read and listen to John 14:1–7.

The Lord's Prayer, James Tissot, 1886–1896

God the Father sent Jesus to us. Jesus is the way to God. Jesus teaches us. When we follow Jesus' teachings, we grow closer to God.

Before he died, Jesus told his friends not to worry. He told them to trust in him. He said God would take care of them. Jesus wants us to trust in him too.

Jesus gave us the Lord's Prayer to remind us of the way to God. The Lord's Prayer tells us that God is our Father. It also helps us ask God for what we need.

Prayer

Jesus, my friend, help me trust God the Father in all things.

Learning the Lord's Prayer

We learned how the Lord's Prayer begins.

Our Father who art in heaven,
hallowed be thy name;
thy kingdom come,
thy will be done
on earth, as it is in heaven.

Now we will learn the rest of the prayer.

Give us this day our daily bread,	We ask God to give us what we need.
and forgive us our ***trespasses,***	We ask God to forgive us for hurting others.
as we forgive those who trespass against us;	We ask God to help us forgive those who have hurt us.
and lead us not into ***temptation,***	We ask God to help us do good. We ask God to help us resist thoughts or feelings that can lead us to disobey him.
but deliver us from evil.	We ask God to protect us from anything that is not pleasing to him.
Amen.	We say yes to God.

Link to Liturgy

We always pray the Lord's Prayer at Mass. Sometimes we sing it. Sometimes we speak it.

ART PRINT 8

Art Print 8 shows a woman giving a kiss to her child. How do you show someone that you are sorry?

Saying We Are Sorry

In the Lord's Prayer, we ask God to forgive us when we hurt others. God forgives us if we are sorry. We can say, "I'm sorry."

In the Lord's Prayer, we also ask God to help us forgive those who have hurt us. We can be like God and forgive the person. We can say, "That's OK. I forgive you."

ACTIVITY: We Forgive

Write *I'm sorry.* in the box on the left.
Write *That's OK. I forgive you.* in the box on the right.

REFLECT

Pray the Lord's Prayer

Prepare yourself for praying the Lord's Prayer. The Lord's Prayer tells us that God is our Father. The Lord's Prayer helps us tell God what we need. As you pray the Lord's Prayer, think about what you are asking God the Father to do for you. Thank him for giving you what you need. Pray the Sign of the Cross. Then pray the words below.

Prayer

Lord's Prayer

Our Father who art in heaven,
hallowed be thy name;
thy kingdom come,
thy will be done
on earth, as it is in heaven.
Give us this day our daily bread,
and forgive us our trespasses,
as we forgive those who trespass
against us;
and lead us not into temptation,
but deliver us from evil.

God Gives Us What We Need

God the Father wants us to have what we need. Think about what you ask God the Father for. What do you really need?

ACTIVITY: Needs or Wants?

Circle the things you really need.

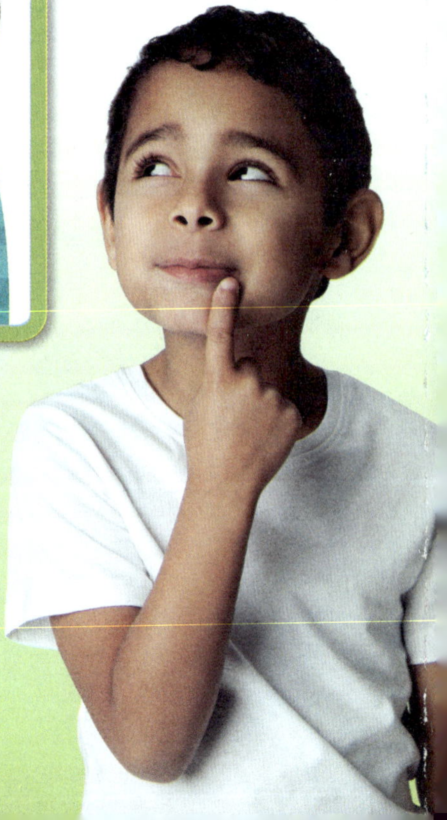

Reading God's Word

Your Father is pleased to give you the kingdom.

Luke 12:32

Living My Faith

Faith Summary

In the Lord's Prayer, we ask God to give us what we need. We ask him to protect us. We ask him to forgive us and to help us forgive others.

Words I Learned

temptation **trespass**

Ways of Being Like Jesus

Jesus asked his Father only for what he truly needed. *Ask God the Father only for what you truly need.*

Prayer

God the Father, thank you for showing me the way to you. Thank you for giving me what I need. Help me trust in you.

ACTIVITY: The Lord's Prayer

Draw a line to correctly complete each part of the Lord's Prayer.

Give us this day our ______________ •	• trespasses,
and forgive us our ______________ •	• into temptation,
as we forgive those who __________ •	• daily bread,
and lead us not ______________ •	• evil. Amen.
but deliver us from ______________ •	• trespass against us;

With My Family

Scripture Together

When we feel thankful, we tell people. The writer of a song in the Book of Isaiah tells how wonderful it feels to trust in a good and loving God.

As a family, read this song of thanks in Isaiah 12:2–4. When you have finished, discuss the Scripture. You may use the following questions to prompt discussion:

- Why is the writer unafraid?
- What would you say in a song of thanks to God?
- How can you help our family to show trust in God?

Family Prayer

Pray together:

Dear God, thank you for the many blessings you grant our family. We trust you to show us the way. Amen.

Faith on the Go

Ask one another: *What is one thing you need from God every day?*

ACTIVITY: Develop a Thankful Attitude

Take turns sharing one thing each family member is thankful for today. Make a list in the form of a prayer, such as "God our Father, we thank you for ____." Attach the prayer to the refrigerator so everyone can read the prayer as a reminder to be thankful.

Jesus Rises from the Dead

SESSION 9

GOD'S WORD

Read and listen to John 20:1–9.

The Women at the Sepulchre, illustration from *Women of the Bible,* published by the Religious Tract Society, 1927

Jesus had many friends when he lived on earth. His close friends were called disciples because they followed Jesus. They tried to live like him. Jesus taught them many lessons. The disciples did not always know what Jesus meant.

When Jesus died, the disciples were sad. They felt alone. They went to his tomb, but it was empty. They were frightened.

One disciple remembered what Jesus had taught them. Jesus would rise from the dead. Now the disciple knew what Jesus meant. Jesus was not dead. Jesus was risen. He was with them!

Prayer

Dear Jesus, help me understand your teachings. Thank you for always being with me.

Jesus Is Risen

Two women went to Jesus' tomb. The rock was moved away from the entrance. An angel sat on the rock. The women were scared. The angel told them not to be afraid. He knew they were looking for Jesus.

The angel said Jesus was not in the tomb. Jesus was risen from the dead. This is what Jesus said would happen.

The women looked inside the tomb and saw it was true. They were full of joy! They knew Jesus **Christ** was alive. They ran to tell Jesus' close followers, the **disciples.**

On the way to the disciples, the women saw Jesus Christ. He was walking on the road. The women were so happy! They cried with joy. Jesus spoke to them.

> "Do not be afraid. Go tell my brothers to go to Galilee, and there they will see me."
>
> *Matthew 28:10*

Reading God's Word

[Jesus said,] "For where two or three are gathered together in my name, there am I in the midst of them."

Matthew 18:20

ART PRINT 9

Art Print 9 shows the risen Jesus Christ surrounded by his friends. How can you share the Easter message that Christ is risen?

Jesus Is Alive!

Jesus Christ rose from the dead. We call this the **Resurrection.** We celebrate Jesus Christ's Resurrection at Easter.

Jesus' friends remembered all that he had taught them. They knew Jesus was with them when they prayed. Jesus is with us, too, when we pray. It's good to know that Jesus is with us always.

ACTIVITY: Jesus Is with Me Always

Finish each sentence with the correct word from the word box.

playground	**Mass**	**school**	**asleep**	**pray**

Jesus is with me . . .

1. in the morning when I get ready for ______________________.
2. when I play with my friends on the ______________________.
3. when I fold my hands, close my eyes, and ______________________.
4. at night when my eyes are closed and I'm ______________________.
5. when I go to church for ______________________.

Link to Liturgy

Catholics around the world celebrate Jesus' Resurrection at Mass.

Be with Jesus

Jesus is always with you. He is with you when you are happy. He is with you when you are sad. He is with you when you think about him. He is with you when you pray. Meet Jesus in your heart. Be with Jesus as you pray the prayer below.

Prayer

Dear Jesus, I like talking with you. I know that you are with me every hour of every day. I am joyful to have you so close to me. Thank you for always being with me.

Jesus Brings New Life

Jesus rose from the dead so we could have new life with God the Father. Jesus' Resurrection brings us hope and joy.

ACTIVITY: Finding Jesus

Help the women find the tomb. Then help them find Jesus Christ.

Living My Faith

Faith Summary

Jesus' friends were sad when he died. Then they found out that Jesus had risen. Jesus was alive! Jesus' friends prayed together.

Prayer

Jesus, my friend, thank you for bringing new life through your Death and Resurrection.

Words I Learned

Christ **disciple** **Resurrection**

Ways of Being Like Jesus

Jesus is always here with us. *Take time to talk to Jesus and listen to him in your heart.*

ACTIVITY: Jesus and You

Circle the true statements below.

Jesus is with me when I need him.

Jesus is too busy for me sometimes.

Jesus is only with me when I am happy.

Jesus is with me when I am afraid.

Jesus is always with me.

With My Family

Scripture Together

After the Resurrection, Jesus appeared to two of his friends on a road. They were sad because Jesus had died. At first they did not know Jesus. They recognized Jesus that evening when he blessed bread, broke it, and gave it to them.

As a family, read about Jesus meeting his disciples in Luke 24:13–35. When you have finished, discuss the Scripture. You may use the following questions to prompt discussion:

- What does Jesus explain as he walks with his friends?
- What things do you think about as Jesus walks with you?
- How do you help our family walk with Jesus?

Family Prayer

Pray together:
Dear Jesus, help us walk with you. Let us be loving and caring with everyone we meet. Amen.

Faith on the Go

Ask one another: *Where do you like to go to talk with Jesus?*

ACTIVITY: Surprise Notes

Help one another walk with Jesus. Place notes around the house for family members to find during the week. Each note might express a simple statement such as "Jesus is with you," "I am here for you," or "Pray the Lord's Prayer tonight. Sleep tight!"

Celebrating Advent

SESSION 10

GOD'S WORD

Read and listen to Micah 5:1–3.

St. David's City, Tony Todd, 2005

Long ago, God's people waited. They waited for God the Father to send the Messiah, or Savior. The Messiah would save them.

The people prayed. They looked for signs from God. Holy people called prophets told stories about the Messiah. They said the Messiah would come. People shared these stories for years.

The stories came true. Jesus was born. He came to save us. During Advent, we are joyful. We prepare to celebrate. We prepare for the birth of Jesus. He is the Messiah.

Prayer

Dear God, during Advent prepare my heart for the arrival of your Son, Jesus.

We Prepare During Advent

We celebrate **Advent** each liturgical year. Advent is a season. It begins four Sundays before Christmas. Advent is a time to prepare.

Advent reminds us that baby Jesus is coming soon. Jesus is the **Messiah,** or Savior. We get ready. We prepare our hearts for Jesus. We are helpful and kind. We love and forgive others. We say we are sorry. We pray more often. We are joyful. We get excited.

ACTIVITY: Prepare for Jesus

How will you prepare your heart for Jesus? Write two ways.

1. ______________________________

____

2. ______________________________

____

____

Reading God's Word

The love of God was revealed to us: God sent his only Son into the world so that we might have life through him.

I John 4:9

Mass During Advent

We go to Mass during Advent. You may see an Advent wreath in church. The wreath has four candles. Three candles are violet. One candle is rose.

What We Experience

We light one candle the first week of Advent. We light one more candle each week. The wreath gets brighter and brighter. The bright light stands for Jesus. Jesus is the **Light of the World.** Jesus helps us see how much God the Father loves us.

ACTIVITY: Light of the World

Color the Advent wreath and the candles.

Link to Liturgy

We do not sing the *Gloria* on Sundays during Advent.

ART PRINT
10

Art Print 10 shows Mary and Joseph's journey to Bethlehem before Jesus' birth. What can you do to welcome Jesus into your heart?

Celebrating Advent

The Advent season begins four Sundays before Christmas. During Advent we prepare to celebrate Jesus' birth. At church we light the candles of the Advent wreath. Each week, one more candle is lit. The light becomes brighter as Jesus' birth nears.

ACTIVITY: I Prepare for Jesus

Imagine that Jesus is coming to be a guest in your home. How will you get ready? How will you spend your time with him? Write your sentences below.

Living My Faith

Faith Summary

Advent is a time to get ready to celebrate Jesus' birth. During each day of Advent, we get ready to welcome Jesus into our hearts.

Prayer

Dear Jesus, we are so happy and thankful that you are coming!

Words I Learned

Advent **Light of the World** **Messiah**

Ways of Being Like Jesus

Jesus loves and welcomes everyone. *Invite a new friend over to play.*

ACTIVITY: Advent Prayer

Trace the letters. Color the candle violet. Color the flame red. Then pray the prayer on the Advent candle.

AT HOME

With My Family

Scripture Together

During Advent, we prepare to celebrate Jesus' birth. We prepare to welcome Jesus. We also prepare for the time when Jesus will come again. We are patient as we make our hearts ready for Jesus' arrival.

Family Prayer

Pray together:

Dear God, help us prepare to welcome your Son, Jesus. Amen.

As a family, read about the need for patience in James 5:7–8. When you have finished, discuss the Scripture. You may use the following questions to prompt discussion:

- How does being patient help farmers?
- How has being patient helped you?
- How can you show patience with our family?

Faith on the Go

Ask one another: *What will you do this Advent to prepare for Christmas?*

ACTIVITY: Family Advent Wreath

Set up an Advent wreath to help one another grow in faith. Take time each week to light the candles and pray together as a family. Talk about how you are preparing your heart for Jesus' coming.

UNIT 3

The Church, Our Community in the Spirit

UNIT 3

The Church, Our Community in the Spirit

Saint Peter

Peter was fishing with other fishermen. Jesus called and said, "Come after me, and I will make you fishers of men." So Peter left his work. He followed Jesus.

Peter loved Jesus and tried to be like him. But at times Peter made bad choices. He did not always do the right thing. Jesus forgave Peter each time.

Jesus had many friends. They followed him. Jesus asked Peter to care for them. Peter said yes. Jesus made Peter their leader. Peter cared for Jesus' followers.

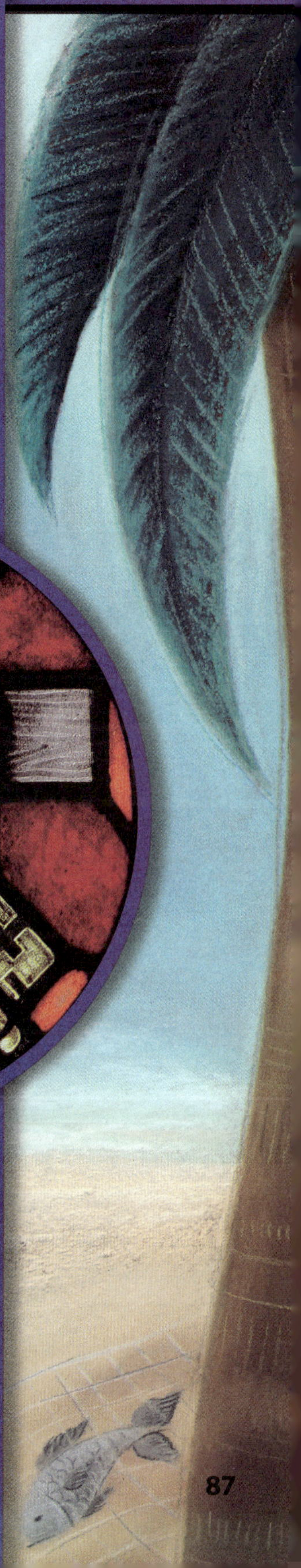

Be Inspired

Lord, you know everything; you know that I love you.

John 21:17

Say Yes to God

Saint Peter chose to follow Jesus. Peter tried to be like Jesus, but it was not always easy. Peter learned from Jesus how to show God's love.

God calls us to follow his Son, Jesus, too. Like Peter, we can say yes to God. We can delight in doing God's will. We can try to be like Jesus. We can show God's love to others.

Reading God's Word

I delight to do your will, my God.
Psalm 40:9

ACTIVITY: Follow Jesus

Trace the letters and read the sentence. Then color the footprint.

Following Jesus

SESSION 11

GOD'S WORD

Read and listen to Luke 5:1–11.

Jesus' friends watched him. They saw him care for others. They saw him help others. Jesus called his friends to follow him. These friends were Jesus' first disciples.

After Jesus rose from the dead, he came to his disciples. He told them to teach others. The disciples went to many lands. They shared Jesus' message of love.

Today Jesus' disciples are all around the world. We are Jesus' disciples. We try to be like Jesus. We show God's love to others.

Jesus and the fishermen

Prayer

Jesus, I hear your invitation to be your friend. Show me how to follow you.

The Church

Jesus' followers are called the **Church.** Jesus gives us the Church as a sign of his love. Jesus loves everyone in the world. We form one body, the Catholic Church. The word **catholic** means "all over the world." The Church is catholic because Jesus' followers are all over the world.

Jesus is the head of the Church. Catholics follow Jesus together. We learn to love one another. We learn to love others in the world. The Holy Spirit helps us. He unites us with God the Father. He fills us with God's peace and love.

India

Philippines

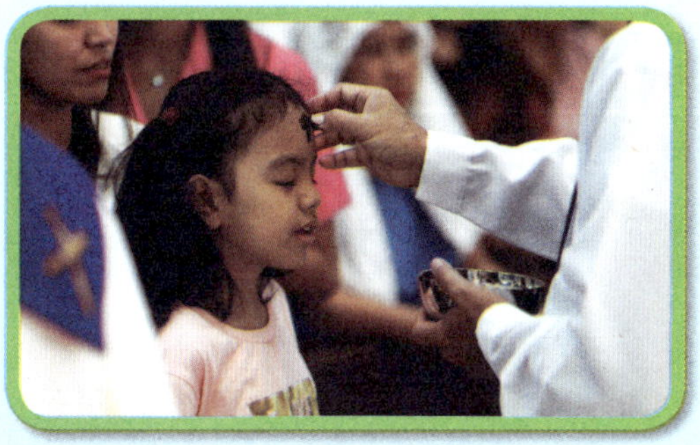

Mexico

Haiti

The Church has angels watching over it. You have your very own angel. You have a **guardian angel.** This angel guards you. It watches over you. It guides you. It helps you grow closer to God.

ACTIVITY: My Guardian Angel

Draw a picture of your guardian angel. Remember that this angel guards you.

Meet a Saint

Saint Michael is an archangel, an angel of the highest rank. He cares for police officers and for our Church. You have an angel caring for you too.

ART PRINT 11

Art Print 11 shows Jesus calling Andrew and Peter to follow him. How can you be a good friend to Jesus and to others?

Jesus Asks Friends to Follow

One day Peter and his brother Andrew were fishing. Jesus passed by. He said to them,

> "Come after me, and I will make you fishers of men."
>
> *Mark 1:17*

Peter and Andrew left their work and followed Jesus. Then Jesus spoke to James and John. Jesus asked them to follow him. James and John left their work to follow Jesus too.

Jesus Asks Us to Follow

Today, Jesus asks us to follow him. Peter, Andrew, James, and John were good friends to Jesus. We need good friends too. In the Church we can find friends who follow Jesus.

ACTIVITY: We Follow Jesus

Draw a picture of yourself with your friends.

Pray to Follow Jesus

Think about how Jesus called the fishermen to follow him. Then open your heart and mind to pray and reflect on the prayer below.

Prayer

Imagine you are playing. You hear someone call your name. You look up. It is Jesus. He asks you to follow him. He asks, "Will you help me? Help me show God's love to others." Spend some time with Jesus. Trust him to lead you. How will you answer Jesus?

Jesus, I say yes. I am happy to follow you. Please show me the way as I share God the Father's love with others.

People in Your Church

People who follow Jesus are the Church. Jesus' followers make up the Body of Christ.

ACTIVITY: The Body of Christ

Draw Jesus' followers in church. Be sure to draw yourself too.

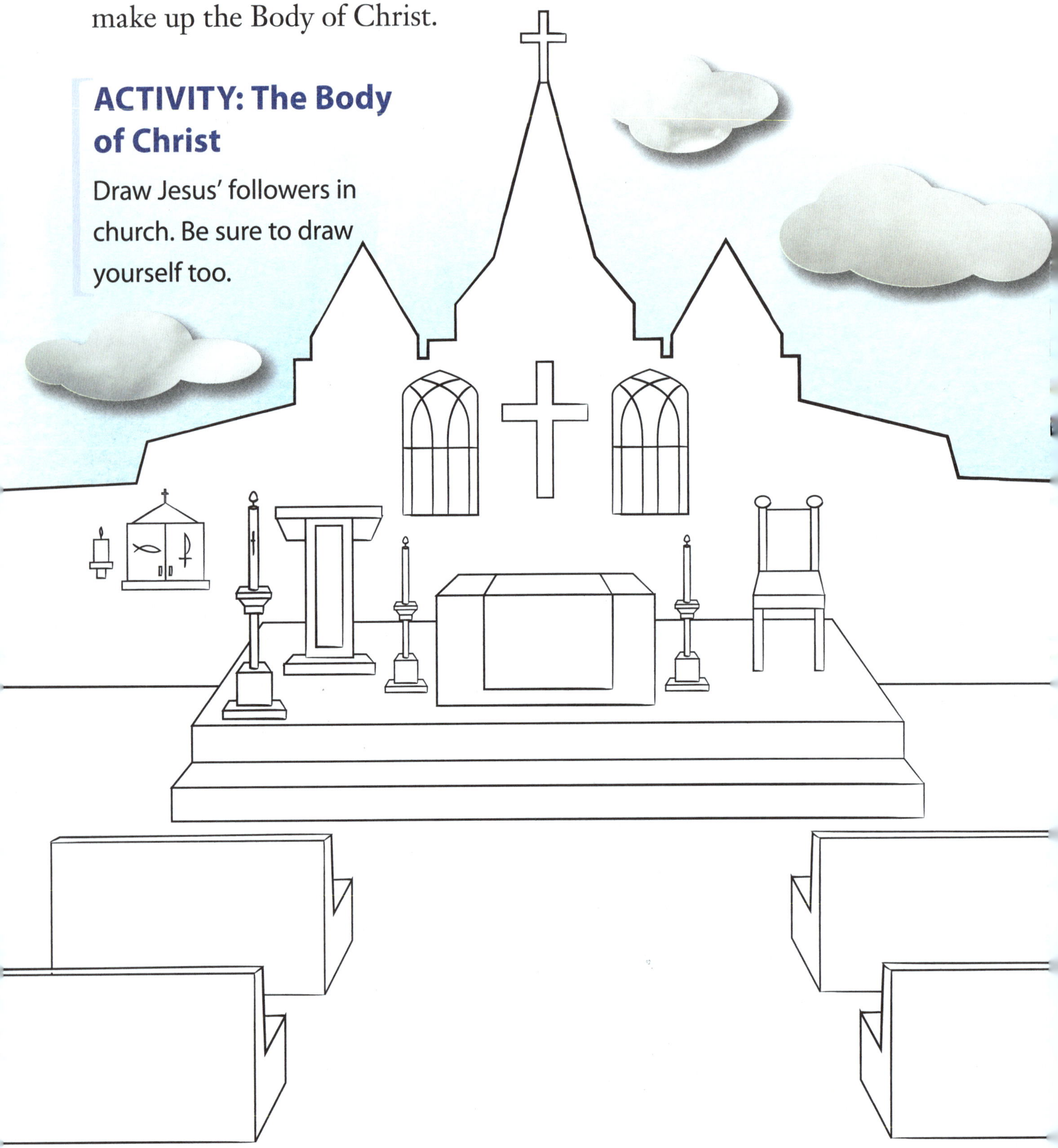

Living My Faith

Faith Summary

Jesus calls us to be part of the Church. We find Jesus' friends in church. We find love and friendship through the Church.

Words I Learned

catholic **guardian angel**
Church

Ways of Being Like Jesus

Jesus cares for us and helps us. *Teach your friends how to show God's love to others. Set a good example and be nice to everyone.*

Prayer

Dear Jesus, I will answer your call.

ACTIVITY: Jesus Calls You!

Jesus calls you to follow him. Write your name to finish the sentence. Then color the fish.

AT HOME

With My Family

Scripture Together

Jesus chose his friends, the Twelve Apostles, to help him teach others about God. Jesus told them to take no food or money with them. The Twelve did as Jesus instructed. They had faith and trust in God to provide for their needs.

As a family, read about Jesus' first followers in **Mark 6:7–13**. When you have finished, discuss the Scripture. You may use the following questions to prompt discussion:

- What did Jesus call for the Twelve to do when they entered a house?
- What person, cause, or event calls you to make a positive difference in the lives of others?
- How can you answer God's call in our church or community?

Family Prayer

Pray together:
Dear Jesus, help our family as we follow the example of the Twelve. Amen.

Faith on the Go

Ask one another: *How can you forgive or heal others or give up attachments to possessions?*

ACTIVITY: Greet Jesus' Friends

Stay for a few minutes after Mass this Sunday to talk with members of the Church whom you do not know. Introduce yourselves and learn something about your new friends.

Jesus Sends the Holy Spirit

SESSION 12

GOD'S WORD

Read and listen to 2 Corinthians 13:11–13.

The Holy Spirit

God the Father invites us. He invites all people. God loves us all!

His Son, Jesus, wants all of us to know the Father's love. Jesus wants us to share his Father's love.

We receive the Holy Spirit in Baptism. The Holy Spirit guides us. He makes us strong and gives us peace. He fills us with joy. The Holy Spirit unites us as followers of Jesus. We rejoice as we share God's love with others.

Prayer

Come, Holy Spirit.

The Holy Spirit Is with Us

God the Father, God the Son, and God the Holy Spirit are the Holy Trinity. Just as God the Father and Jesus the Son love and care for us, so does the Holy Spirit. All Three Persons of the Holy Trinity love and care for us.

The Holy Spirit comes to us in Baptism. He guides us. He helps us be kind. He helps us be caring.

The Holy Spirit is with us always. He is with us at home and at school. He is with us in our **parish.** A parish is a community of Jesus' followers. Our parish is part of the Catholic Church. The people of our parish worship God together in our church. The people of our parish also serve one another.

Did You Know?

The Holy Spirit is like the wind. We cannot see him, but we know he is with us always. We can feel him as he guides us to do the right thing.

The Holy Spirit leads us. He reveals God's Word as the truth. The Holy Spirit guides us to do what is right.

ACTIVITY: Live by the Holy Spirit

Color the words that tell how the Holy Spirit helps us act.

Lovingly

Kindly

Holy Spirit

Courageously

ART PRINT 12

Art Print 12 shows Jesus' friends receiving the Holy Spirit. How do you feel knowing that the Holy Spirit is with you?

The Holy Spirit Comes

As told in Acts of the Apostles, one day, Jesus' friends were praying. Whoosh! A big wind came from the sky. It filled the house. They saw flames of fire, but they were not afraid. The Holy Spirit had come. Now they could tell the world about Jesus. We call this special day **Pentecost.**

The Holy Spirit Brings Courage

Before this day, Jesus' friends were afraid of people who did not like them. But then the Holy Spirit came. He gave them courage. They were not afraid to talk about Jesus anymore.

ACTIVITY: Signs of the Holy Spirit

Color the symbols of the Holy Spirit on this page.

Reading God's Word

The fruit of the Spirit is love, joy, peace.

Galatians 5:22

Pray to the Holy Spirit

Think of a kind thing you did. The Holy Spirit helped you be kind. We can pray to the Holy Spirit. Pray the prayer below.

Prayer

The Holy Spirit lives in your heart. Talk with him. Thank him for being your friend. Ask him to help you be more loving.

Sign of the Cross

In the name of the Father
and of the Son
and of the Holy Spirit.

God the Holy Spirit

The Holy Spirit surprised Jesus' disciples. They did not expect his visit. They did not expect the wonderful gift the Holy Spirit brought them.

ACTIVITY: The Story of the Holy Spirit

Finish the story. Use the words in the box. Look at the pictures for help.

disciples	**fire**	**Jesus**	**praying**	**wind**

1. One day Jesus' ______________________________ were together.

2. They were ______________________________.

3. A big ______________________________ came from the sky.

4. They saw flames of ______________________________, but they were not afraid.

5. Then they told the world about

______________________________.

Living My Faith

Faith Summary

The Holy Spirit is always with us. He helps us be kind. He helps us be loving.

Words I Learned

parish **Pentecost**

Ways of Being Like Jesus

Jesus gives us the Holy Spirit. This shows Jesus' unending kindness. *Do a kind deed. Help someone with a chore or task without being asked.*

Prayer

Holy Spirit, fill my heart with love.

ACTIVITY: Loving Actions

Think of someone to whom you can show love in some way. Write that person's name. Then write how you will show your love.

I can show love to

________________________.

I will show my love by

____

____

________________________.

With My Family

Scripture Together

After Jesus' Resurrection, his disciples gathered together. Suddenly they heard a loud noise like a strong wind. The Holy Spirit came to them. He helped them speak in many languages. People from every nation understood them.

Family Prayer

Pray together:
Come, Holy Spirit. Guide our thoughts and our deeds. Amen.

As a family, read about Jesus' friends being filled with the Holy Spirit in **Acts of the Apostles 2:1–6**. When you have finished, discuss the Scripture. You may use the following questions to prompt discussion:

- How did the Holy Spirit come to the disciples?
- What can the gift of the Holy Spirit help you do as a disciple?
- How can you help others understand God's message?

Faith on the Go

Ask one another: *How can you thank the Holy Spirit for always being with you?*

ACTIVITY: Opening up to the Holy Spirit

Go outside and find a place to sit. Close your eyes and breathe deeply in and out. Feel the warmth of the sun. Feel the wind. Listen to the sounds around you. Open your heart to the presence of the Holy Spirit. Take turns praying, asking for help with something. Ask the Holy Spirit to give you courage, joy, and peace.

Jesus Teaches Us to Share

SESSION 13

GOD'S WORD

Read and listen to Luke 19:1–10.

Jesus summoning Zacchaeus the publican to entertain him at his house, William Brassey Hole, 1846–1917

Jesus shared God's love with everyone. He even loved people who were unkind and hurt others. Jesus forgave them. He welcomed them. Like Zacchaeus, they changed their ways. They chose to follow Jesus and share his love.

We are followers of Jesus too. We believe God is our Father. We believe Jesus his Son came to show us how to live. We believe the Holy Spirit guides us. We believe the Church is God's family.

During Mass we stand and pray together. We pray what we believe. Then we go out and share God's love.

Prayer

Jesus, help me follow you and show others your love.

Sharing with Others

We learn this story in Acts of the Apostles. After the Holy Spirit came, Jesus' friends were happy. They were ready to share Jesus' love.

They lived in a community. They ate and prayed together. They shared everything they had. They shared stories about Jesus. People in the community loved this way of life. Every day more people joined them.

Reading God's Word

In the same way you also should rejoice and share your joy with me.

Philippians 2:18

Who We Are

People who want to live as Jesus Christ taught us to live are called **Christians.** The word *Christian* comes from the word *Christ.* We Catholics are Christians.

As Catholics we share and pray together. Jesus' followers did this long ago. Jesus' followers still do this today.

Jesus shared his peace with his friends. He said to them, "Peace be with you." We share Jesus' peace at Mass. We offer the **Sign of Peace.** We reach out to people near us. We say to them, "Peace be with you."

ACTIVITY: Share at Mass

Look at the pictures. What are the children sharing? Trace the letters to find the answer.

Peace

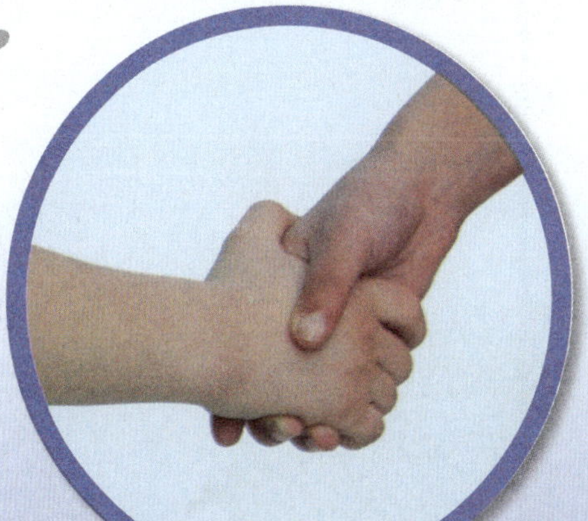

ART PRINT 13

Art Print 13 shows a group of people riding on the subway. How can you show the people around you that you care about them?

Our Neighbors

Who are our neighbors? They are the people around us. God wants us to love them. We show them love by sharing with them. This is what Jesus did.

ACTIVITY: I Care for Others

Complete the sentence below. Then draw a picture of how you feel when you share with others.

I can share by ______________________________

____

____.

Pray to Jesus

Jesus calls us to follow him. He wants us to live as he taught us to live. He wants us to share his love. He wants us to pray together. We can pray to Jesus using the words of Saint Richard below.

Prayer

Thank you, Jesus.
My friend! My brother!
Help me know you more clearly.
Help me love you more dearly.
Help me follow you more nearly.

Now, imagine you are with Jesus. He is smiling at you. Tell Jesus how you will love him. Tell him how you will follow him.

What Can You Share?

Jesus wants us to share his love with others. We can share with our family. We can share with our community.

ACTIVITY: Share God's Love

Draw a picture in each box of something you can share.

I can share with my family.

I can share with my friends.

I can share with my neighbors.

I can share at Mass.

Living My Faith

Faith Summary

We belong to the Catholic Church. We show our love by sharing with others.

Prayer

Loving Jesus, thank you for teaching me how to share.

Words I Learned

Christian **Sign of Peace**

Ways of Being Like Jesus

Jesus shared what he had. *Share a favorite toy or treat with a brother, sister, or friend.*

ACTIVITY: We Believe

Complete each sentence. Use words from the word box.

Catholic	Christians	Peace	share

1. We belong to the ______________________ Church.
2. We can offer a Sign of ______________________ at Mass.
3. Jesus' friends ______________________ with others.
4. ______________________ are followers of Jesus Christ.

With My Family

Scripture Together

Jesus often told stories to teach people lessons. Jesus told the story of the Good Samaritan when someone asked him, "Who is my neighbor?" In the story, Jesus teaches what one person did when he saw someone in need.

As a family, read Jesus' story about the Good Samaritan in **Luke 10:29–37**. When you have finished, discuss the Scripture. You may use the following questions to prompt discussion:

- Why does the Samaritan stop to help the traveler?
- What does the story teach about who your neighbor is?
- How does Jesus want you to treat people you meet even if you do not know them?

Family Prayer

Pray together:
Dear God, help us always show love to our neighbors. Amen.

Faith on the Go

Ask one another: *How can you share your love with others—even people you do not know?*

ACTIVITY: Reach Out to Others

Talk about people in need within your community. Choose one person, family, or cause. Then reach out and help, sharing whatever you can to improve the situation.

God Chooses Mary

SESSION 14

GOD'S WORD

Read and listen to John 2:1–11.

The wedding at Cana

Mary was at a wedding in Cana. Her Son, Jesus, and his disciples were there. Mary noticed that the wine would run out soon. She wanted to help. She asked Jesus to help. She believed in her Son. She told the servers to do what Jesus said. They filled six stone jars with water. Jesus performed his first miracle. He changed the water into the best wine.

Mary in heaven sees our needs too. She wants to help us. She loves and prays for us. She asks her Son, Jesus, to help.

Prayer

Holy Mary, Mother of God, pray for us.

God Loves Mary

God chose Mary to be Jesus' mother.

Mary said she wanted to serve God. Mary said yes to God.

God gave Mary the gift of **grace.** God's grace helped Mary have faith and trust in God.

We can say yes to God too. God's grace helps us have faith and trust in him.

Reading God's Word

"God resists the proud,
but gives grace to the humble."
James 4:6

The Mother of God

Mary knew Jesus was coming. She was the first to know. Jesus is God the Son. We call Mary the Mother of God. Mary loved her Son, Jesus, very much. She loves us too.

Sacred Site

Many Catholic churches have a statue of Mary. Can you find one in your church?

ART PRINT
14

Art Print 14 shows the angel Gabriel visiting Mary. How can you say yes to God like Mary did?

An Angel Visits Mary

As told in the Gospel according to Luke, Mary lived long ago. One day an angel came to her. The angel's name was Gabriel. God sent Gabriel to Mary to give her a message.

Gabriel said, "Do not be afraid. You will have a son. You will name him Jesus."

Mary said, "I will do what God wants." Mary said yes to God.

ACTIVITY: Mary Says Yes

Color the picture of Mary and the angel Gabriel.

REFLECT

Prayer for Mary

Mary is the Mother of God. Mary is also called the Mother of the Church. Prepare yourself to pray the Hail Mary. Pray the Sign of the Cross. Then pray the words below.

Prayer

Hail Mary

Hail, Mary, full of grace,
the Lord is with thee.
Blessed art thou among women
and blessed is the fruit of thy
womb, Jesus.
Holy Mary, Mother of God,
pray for us sinners,
now and at the hour of our death.

Now, think about the words you prayed. Tell Mary you are glad she said yes to God.

Mary Answers God

God chose Mary to be the mother of his Son, Jesus. Mary loved God. She answered God's call.

ACTIVITY: Answer God's Call

What did Mary say to God? Color all the pieces marked with a *Y* blue. Then color the other pieces different colors.

Living My Faith

Faith Summary

God chose Mary to be the mother of Jesus. Mary said yes to God.

Word I Learned

grace

Ways of Being Like Jesus

Jesus loves his mother, Mary. *Show your love for your family. Say yes to God and to your family.*

Prayer

Jesus, thank you for helping me grow in grace. Help me say yes to God each day.

ACTIVITY: I Say Yes

Answer God's call. Write what you will say to God. Then think of a way to show your love to someone in your family. Draw a picture of it.

God, I say ____________.

With My Family

Scripture Together

After Mary said yes to God, she visited her cousin Elizabeth. Mary was filled with joy. She wanted to share the exciting news of God having blessed her so greatly. Mary praises God in a beautiful prayer that is sometimes called the *Magnificat*.

As a family, read Mary's words in **Luke 1:46–55**. When you have finished, discuss the Scripture. You may use the following questions to prompt discussion:

- How do you know Mary was joyful about saying yes to God?
- What example would you add to this prayer to further proclaim the greatness of God?
- How can you help our family show joy when serving God?

Family Prayer

Pray together:
Hail, Mary, full of grace,
the Lord is with thee.
Amen.

Faith on the Go

Ask one another: *What great thing has God done for you recently?*

ACTIVITY: A Decade a Day

Pray the Rosary together as a family. Take turns so every family member has an opportunity to lead with at least one decade.

Celebrating Christmas

SESSION 15

GOD'S WORD

Read and listen to Luke 2:8–14.

Angels are messengers from God. We read about angels in the Bible. An angel told Mary that God chose her. An angel helped Joseph keep the Holy Family safe. An angel told shepherds about the birth of Jesus. The angels sang a joyful song!

Mary, Jesus, the shepherds, and an angel

We hear part of the angels' song at Mass. It is called the *Gloria*. Sometimes we sing the *Gloria*. Sometimes we pray it. We do not pray it on Sundays in Advent or Lent. These are times when we wait and prepare. During the season of Christmas, we joyfully sing the *Gloria*.

Prayer

Glory to God in the highest,
and on earth peace to people
of good will.

EXPLORE

We Celebrate During Christmas

We celebrate **Christmas** on December 25. The season of Christmas begins on Christmas Eve, December 24. It ends on the Feast of the Baptism of the Lord, in January.

Jesus is the **Son of God.** We celebrate Jesus' birth at Christmas. Jesus came to show us how much God the Father loves us. Jesus came to save us.

ACTIVITY: Son of God Word Search

Find and circle the words from the word box.

Christmas God Jesus save

F	H	C	E	P	G	O	D
V	U	H	A	I	T	H	F
A	C	R	R	J	M	Y	B
J	I	I	M	I	E	R	U
E	R	S	A	I	S	E	R
S	O	T	L	E	S	N	U
U	A	M	B	O	I	I	L
S	A	A	K	S	A	V	E
N	D	S	U	F	T	B	A

Reading God's Word

A savior has been born for you.

Luke 2:11

Mass During Christmas

During the Christmas season, we celebrate at Mass. We are joyful about the birth of Jesus. We think about God the Father's gift. We welcome Jesus into our hearts.

What We Experience

The church is bright and colorful. We see trees, wreaths, and lights. We see statues of Mary and Joseph. We also see baby Jesus in a manger. The **celebrant,** a priest or bishop, wears white vestments. We pray together. We sing joyful songs about Jesus' birth.

ACTIVITY: Nativity Scene

Color the picture of the Nativity scene.

Did You Know?

Some churches have a "living" Nativity scene. Real people and animals are in the scene.

ART PRINT 15

Art Print 15 shows baby Jesus with Mary, Joseph, shepherds, angels, and animals. How can you spread the joy of Christmas all year long?

Celebrating Christmas

Christmas begins on Christmas Eve, December 24, and ends on the Sunday after the Feast of the Epiphany in January.

Three Wise Men believed that someday a star would tell of the birth of the Son of God. They waited to see the star in the sky. When it finally came, they packed their camels with gifts. They traveled for almost a year to reach Jesus. The Wise Men's long trip to see Jesus showed how important his birth was.

The Gift of Jesus

Jesus is the most important gift of Christmas. Jesus taught us to love God most of all. Jesus taught us to love one another.

ACTIVITY: My Prayer of Thanks

Write a prayer thanking God for giving us Jesus. Ask God to bless you and your family.

Living My Faith

Faith Summary

Christmas is a time to celebrate the birth of Jesus. Jesus is the Son of God who came to save us.

Prayer

Dear Jesus, help me remember we celebrate you during this season.

Words I Learned

celebrant **Christmas** **Son of God**

Ways of Being Like Jesus

Jesus brought joy to the world. *Share your joy this Christmas. Sing a Christmas carol to remind others of Jesus' birth.*

ACTIVITY: Joyful Angels

Color the words the angels sang. Draw angels around the words.

Glory to God in the highest!

With My Family

Scripture Together

The Magi traveled from the East to honor Jesus. On their way, they met King Herod. He was worried by the news of another king. Herod wanted the Magi to come to him after visiting Jesus. The Magi were warned in a dream to go home another way.

Family Prayer

Pray together:

End a meal by asking each family member to read part of the Nativity story from Luke 2:1–19 or Matthew 2:1–12. Conclude the reading by praying together *Amen*.

As a family, read about the Magi's visit to baby Jesus in **Matthew 2:8–12**. When you have finished, discuss the Scripture. You may use the following questions to prompt discussion:

- What gifts did the Magi give to baby Jesus?
- If you were with the Magi, what would you bring to Jesus?
- How can you honor and praise Jesus during this season?

Faith on the Go

Ask one another: *What is your favorite Christmas tradition?*

ACTIVITY: Who's Who

Visit the Nativity scene at your church as a family, or make your own Nativity scene. Identify each person, angel, and animal in the scene. If you craft your own scene, listen to "We Three Kings" and other Christmas carols as you work.

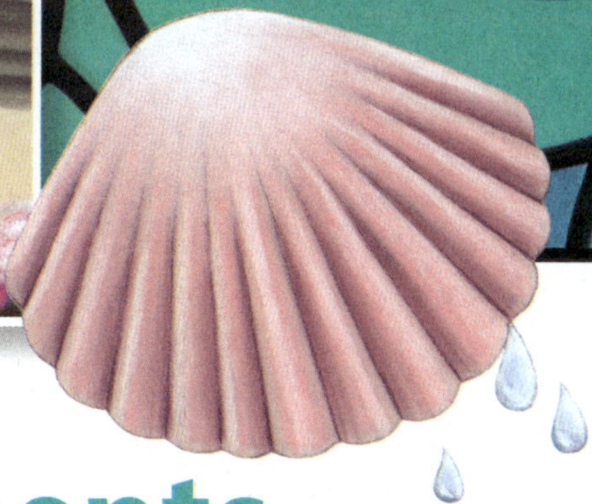

UNIT 4

Sacraments, Our Way of Life

UNIT 4

Sacraments, Our Way of Life

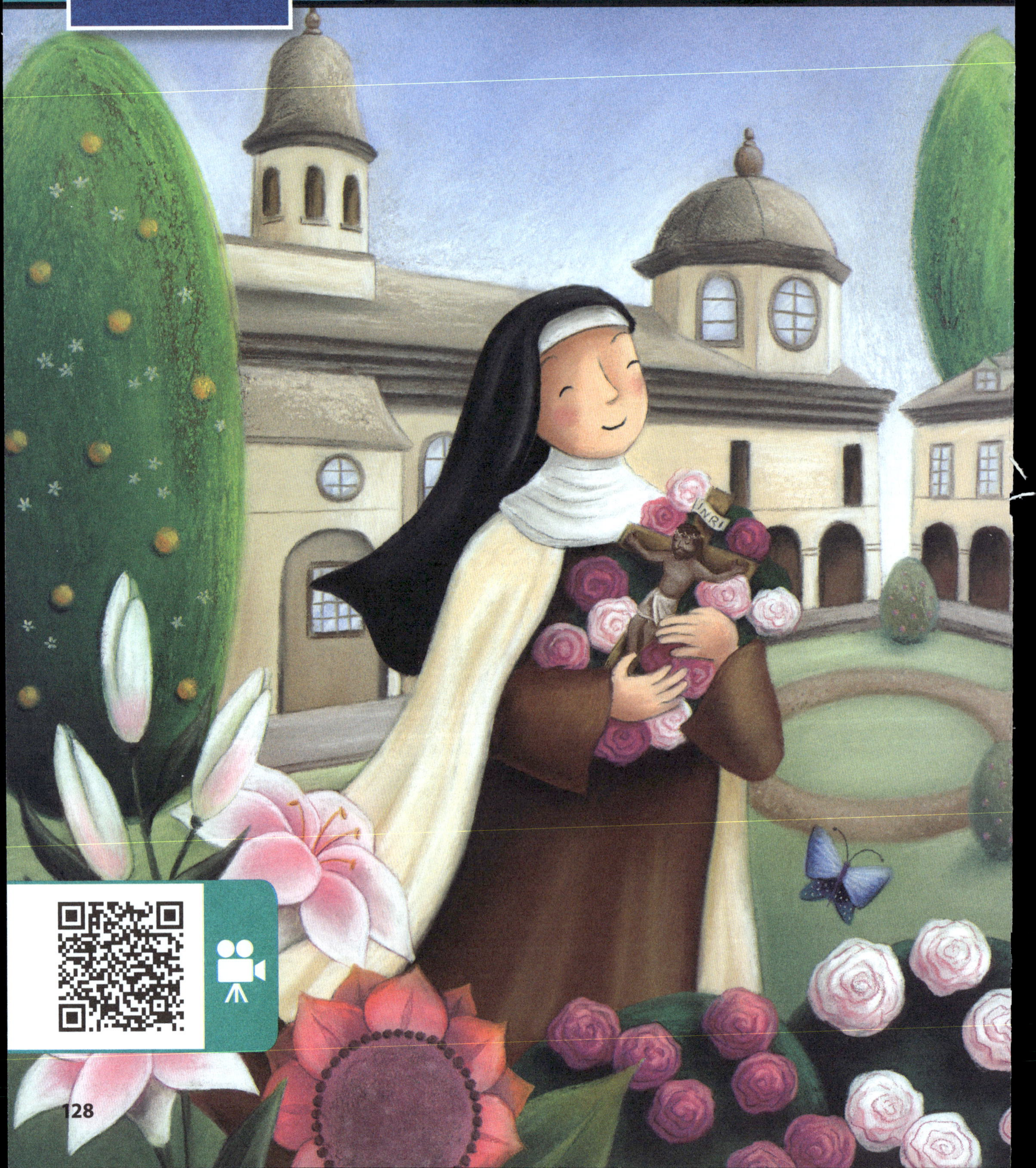

Saint Thérèse of the Child Jesus

Thérèse became a saint by doing her best. She loved God very much. She wanted to do everything for him. When Thérèse was 15 years old, she dedicated her life to God. She became a Carmelite sister.

Thérèse loved flowers. She thought of herself as a "little flower of Jesus." She gave glory to God by doing her best to please God. She did little things every day to show her love for God. She called this her "Little Way."

We can be like Saint Thérèse too. We can always do our best. We can honor God by doing everything with love.

Be Inspired

I want to spend my [time in] heaven doing good on earth.

Saint Thérèse of the Child Jesus

Loving God in Little Ways

Thérèse wanted to please God as a little flower of Jesus. She did little things to show her love for God. She offered every thought and action as a prayer to God. People often call Saint Thérèse the "Little Flower."

We can show our love for God in little ways too. We can make every thought and kind act a prayer to God.

Reading God's Word

I will praise you, LORD, with all my heart.

Psalm 9:2

ACTIVITY: Little Loving Ways

Think of little ways you can show love for Jesus. Write one way next to each flower. Then color the flower.

1. ______________________________

3. ______________________________

2. ______________________________

Jesus in Our Lives

SESSION 16

GOD'S WORD

Read and listen to John 13:34–35.

The First Shall Be the Last, James-Jacques-Joseph Tissot, 1886–1894.

While on earth, Jesus loved and cared for people. He did this even when it was not easy. Jesus prayed to God the Father. Jesus asked his Father to give him strength to love everyone. Jesus healed the sick. He fed the hungry. He welcomed everyone. Near the end of his life, Jesus was with his friends. He told them to love one another as he had loved them.

Jesus wants us to love one another too. He wants us to care for others. Loving like Jesus is not always easy, but Jesus helps us. Jesus gives us signs of his love to help us.

Prayer

Jesus, my friend, help me see the signs of your love.

Jesus Loves Us

Jesus gives us signs of his love. We call these signs **sacraments.** They give us God's grace. Grace is God's life that makes us strong and fills us with love.

Three sacraments welcome us into the Church. The **Sacraments of Initiation** are Baptism, Confirmation, and the Eucharist.

There are two **Sacraments of Healing.** One is the Sacrament of Penance and Reconciliation. The other is the Sacrament of the Anointing of the Sick.

Two sacraments help us serve others. The **Sacraments at the Service of Communion** are Matrimony and Holy Orders.

Did You Know?

Jesus gave us the seven sacraments. They help us live the way God wants us to live.

Priests help us celebrate the sacraments. Priests are men who have received the Sacrament of Holy Orders. Priests serve and guide the Church. They share signs of Jesus' love.

ACTIVITY: Group the Sacraments

Read each group of sacraments. Then write the correct word to name the group.

Healing	Initiation	Service of Communion

Baptism
Confirmation
Eucharist
→ Sacraments of ____________________

Matrimony
Holy Orders
→ Sacraments at the ____________________

Penance and Reconciliation
Anointing of the Sick
→ Sacraments of ____________________

Reading God's Word

For by grace you have been saved through faith, and this is not from you; it is the gift of God.

Ephesians 2:8

ART PRINT
16

Art Print 16 shows Jesus surrounded by children. How can you live the way God wants you to live?

Jesus Loves Children

People brought children to see Jesus. However, Jesus' friends said, "Do not bother him with children."

Jesus heard this. He was upset. He said,

> "Let the children come to me; do not prevent them, for the kingdom of God belongs to such as these."
>
> *Mark 10:14*

Jesus hugged the children. Then he blessed them.

ACTIVITY: Signs of Jesus' Love

Jesus loves all children. Look at the picture. How is Jesus showing love? Write your answer below. Then color the picture.

Be with Jesus

Imagine that you are sitting next to Jesus. He puts his hand on your forehead. He blesses you. He smiles at you. He spends time with you. Pray the prayer below to spend time with Jesus.

Prayer

Jesus wants you to know that he loves you. He wants you to know that you are important to him. How does knowing that make you feel? What will you say to Jesus? Will you tell him you love him? Will you thank him?

Be still with Jesus. Tell him what's in your heart. Enjoy being with him.

Time with Jesus

Jesus loves you very much. He loves you when you talk with him. He loves you when you share what is in your heart. Jesus loves you all the time. He loves you just the way you are.

ACTIVITY: A Note to Jesus

Write a note to Jesus. Tell him how much you love him.

Dear Jesus,

Living My Faith

Faith Summary

Jesus gives us signs of his love. We call them sacraments. Sacraments give us grace and fill us with God's love.

Prayer

Thank you, Jesus, for signs that show you are near.

Words I Learned

priest
sacrament
Sacraments at the Service of Communion
Sacraments of Initiation
Sacraments of Healing

Ways of Being Like Jesus

The sacraments are signs of Jesus' love for us. *Show your love for Jesus. When you are sad or angry, try to be kind and helpful.*

ACTIVITY: Love Signs

Jesus tells us to love as he does. On each sign, write the name of someone you love. Then color the signs.

With My Family

Scripture Together

We can know God the Father best by knowing his Son, Jesus. When Jesus teaches about prayer, he compares God's love for us to a parent's love for his or her child. Jesus explains that God loves us and is always with us. God always hears and answers our prayers. His answers may come through Scripture or other people—family, friends, and others whom we trust.

As a family, read about God's desire to hear our prayers in Luke 11:9–13. When you have finished, discuss the Scripture. You may use the following questions to prompt discussion:

- What advice does Jesus give about prayer?
- How can you knock on God's door?
- Through whom has God answered your prayer recently?

Family Prayer

Pray together:
Dear Jesus, thank you for the gifts of your sacraments. Help us share signs of your love every day. Amen.

Faith on the Go

Ask one another: *What has someone done lately to show love for you?*

ACTIVITY: Sharing Signs of Love

Show a family member a sign of your love. Do something kind for him or her.

Joining God's Family

SESSION 17

GOD'S WORD

Read and listen to Matthew 28:16–20.

Mosaic of the Ascension of the Lord, St. Barnabas Church, Bodley and Garner, end of the 19th century

After Jesus rose from the dead, his friends did not know what to do. Jesus called them to a mountain. He gave them a mission. It was an important job.

Jesus told his friends to teach others. He told them to baptize others. He wanted others to join God's family. He wanted others to share God's love.

Jesus gives us a mission too. Through the Sacrament of Baptism we are part of God's family. We joyfully teach others about God. We joyfully share God's love. We show others how to live as children of God.

Prayer

Jesus, guide me to share God the Father's love.

Our First Sacrament

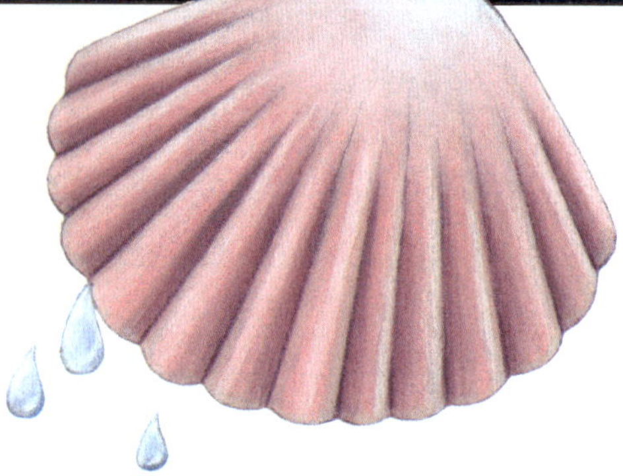

Baptism is a sacrament. It is the first sacrament we celebrate. In Baptism we are welcomed into the Church. We become part of God's family. We become followers of Jesus. The Holy Spirit fills us with new life. We are freed from **Original Sin.** This is the sin that came into the world when Adam and Eve chose not to obey God. Adam and Eve were the first man and woman that God created.

Many of us were baptized as babies. A priest or deacon used blessed water called **holy water.** He poured the holy water on us and said, "I baptize you in the name of the Father, and of the Son, and of the Holy Spirit."

Now we are older. We can bless ourselves. We use holy water to make the Sign of the Cross. The blessing reminds us of our Baptism.

Godparents Are Chosen with Love

Family and friends come to our Baptism. Our parents ask two people to help. They are our **godparents.**

How do godparents help? They help teach us about God. They help us lead good lives. They help us live as followers of Jesus. They pray for us.

Reading God's Word

"Go, therefore, and make disciples of all nations, baptizing them in the name of the Father, and of the Son, and of the holy Spirit."

Matthew 28:19

ART PRINT 17

Art Print 17 shows Saint Peter, one of Jesus' best friends, who called others to follow Jesus. How do we become followers of Jesus?

Followers of Jesus

This story is told in Acts of the Apostles.

One day Peter was talking about Jesus. Many people heard Peter's words. They asked, "How can we follow Jesus?"

"Love God. Join his family," said Peter.

And many did as Peter said. They followed Jesus. They joined God's family.

We Are Invited

Jesus invites us to follow him too. God the Father loves everyone. He wants us to be part of his family. We join God's family when we are baptized.

ACTIVITY: Members of God's Family

Color the two pictures on this page. Remember that you are a member of God's family.

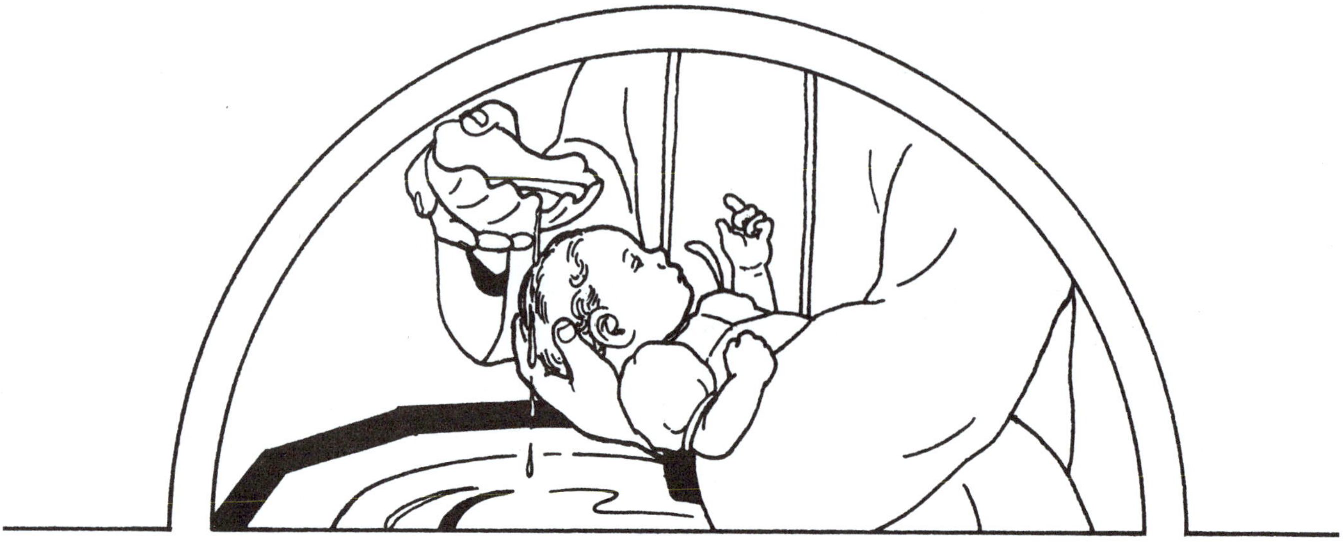

Be a Part of God's Family

Remember: God our Father creates you. Jesus his Son loves you. The Holy Spirit gives you peace. Now, let's pray the prayer below.

Prayer

Baptism welcomes you into God's family. You can show that you are part of his family. You can pray the Sign of the Cross.

Sign of the Cross

In the name of the Father
and of the Son
and of the Holy Spirit.

New Life in Jesus

Baptism begins our new life in God's family. In Baptism, Original Sin is washed away. The Holy Spirit gives us the strength to follow Jesus and to do good.

ACTIVITY: Words of Our First Sacrament

Match each sentence to the correct picture. Write the number in the box.

1. These people help us learn about God.
2. This sacrament makes us followers of Jesus.
3. We bless ourselves with this to remind us of our Baptism.

Holy Water

Baptism

Family

Did You Know?

Every Catholic church has holy water. Where is the holy water in your church?

Living My Faith

Faith Summary

In Baptism we become part of God's family. We receive the Holy Spirit.

Prayer

Jesus, thank you for the gift of Baptism.

Words I Learned

Baptism **godparent** **holy water** **Original Sin**

Ways of Being Like Jesus

Jesus welcomes us into his family at Baptism. *Show how you are part of God's family by acting in loving ways toward others.*

ACTIVITY: The Word of God

We are part of God's family, the Catholic Church. We tell others about God. We share the Word of God. We share God's love.

Draw yourself. Write one thing you can tell someone about God.

With My Family

Scripture Together

After his Resurrection, Jesus sent his followers to teach others about him and make disciples of all nations. The story of the Ethiopian man's Baptism shows Philip carrying out God's plan to welcome everyone.

As a family, read the story of the Ethiopian man in Acts of the Apostles 8:26–38. When you have finished, discuss the Scripture. You may use the following questions to prompt discussion:

- Who told Philip to join up with the chariot on the road to Gaza?
- How do you think Philip felt traveling as far as he did and finding someone who loved God?
- What do you know and love about Jesus that you would share with others?

Family Prayer

Pray together:

Dear God, please bless all our godparents. They have helped us live as you want us to live. Amen.

Faith on the Go

Ask one another: *How can you extend to others the welcome you received in Baptism?*

ACTIVITY: Remember Your Baptism

Gather your family around the holy-water font at church. Dip your fingers in the holy water and pray the Sign of the Cross together to remind yourselves that you are baptized and to show you are part of God's family.

Celebrating Jesus

SESSION 18

GOD'S WORD

Read and listen to John 6:32–35.

Jesus is the Bread of Life.

Jesus teaches us about God the Father's love. God the Father gives us the true bread from heaven. God gave us his only Son, Jesus. Jesus gives us what we need to live. He is as important for life as bread and water. Jesus is the Bread of Life.

The Bread of Life is present for us at Mass when we celebrate the Eucharist. We receive Jesus' Body and Blood in Holy Communion. Jesus, the Bread of Life, is the food that helps us grow closer to God the Father.

Prayer

Jesus, help me give of myself as you have of yourself.

The Last Supper

The night before he died, Jesus was with his friends. They were sharing a meal.

Jesus took bread. He blessed it. He broke it. He shared it with his friends. He said,

> "This is my body, which will be given for you; do this in memory of me."
>
> *Luke 22:19*

Then Jesus took a cup of wine. He blessed it. He shared it with his friends. He said,

> "This cup is the new covenant in my blood, which will be shed for you."
>
> *Luke 22:20*

This meal is called the **Last Supper.** At the Last Supper, Jesus gave his Body and Blood to us.

The Sacrament of the Eucharist

We share a meal with Jesus too. At Mass we celebrate the Sacrament of the **Eucharist.** We also call it Holy Communion. We thank God. We receive God's grace.

During the **consecration,** the priest prays to God. The priest takes wheat bread. He blesses it and says, "This is my Body." Then he takes grape wine. He blesses it and says, "This is my Blood." Jesus now is present under the appearances of bread and wine. What looks and tastes like bread and wine is now the Body and Blood of Jesus Christ.

ACTIVITY: A Special Meal

Match each word in the violet boxes with the words in the blue boxes.

Eucharist	Blood of Jesus Christ
Bread	Body of Jesus Christ
Wine	Holy Communion

ART PRINT 18

Art Print 18 shows many people walking to church for Mass. What is your favorite part of the Mass?

Mass, Our Special Meal

Every Sunday we go to Mass. What do we do at Mass?

- We remember Jesus.
- We have a special meal.
- We show our love for one another.

Before we leave Mass, the priest says important words. He tells us to glorify God by doing good.

ACTIVITY: The Body and Blood of Christ

Color the special meal we have at Mass.

Reading God's Word

Whatever you do, do everything for the glory of God.

I Corinthians 10:31

Mealtime Prayers

We pray the prayer below before we eat. We fold our hands. We think about all that God gives us. We thank God for our food. We thank God for the people around us.

Prayer

Grace Before Meals

Bless us, O Lord, and these thy gifts, which we are about to receive from thy bounty, through Christ our Lord.

We pray the prayer below after we eat. We fold our hands. We think about how blessed we are. We thank God again.

Prayer

Grace After Meals

We give thee thanks, for all thy benefits, Almighty God, who live and reign for ever.

REFLECT

The Blessed Sacrament

Consecrated bread, or hosts, and wine are the **Blessed Sacrament.** Jesus is present in the Blessed Sacrament. After Communion, we put the Blessed Sacrament in the tabernacle. The tabernacle is like a little house. It is near the altar.

We adore Jesus. We remember what he did for us. We show our respect for him. We genuflect or bow in front of the tabernacle.

Chalice with wine and hosts

Genuflecting before entering the pew

ACTIVITY: Jesus Is Here

Draw the hosts and wine inside the tabernacle. Then color the picture.

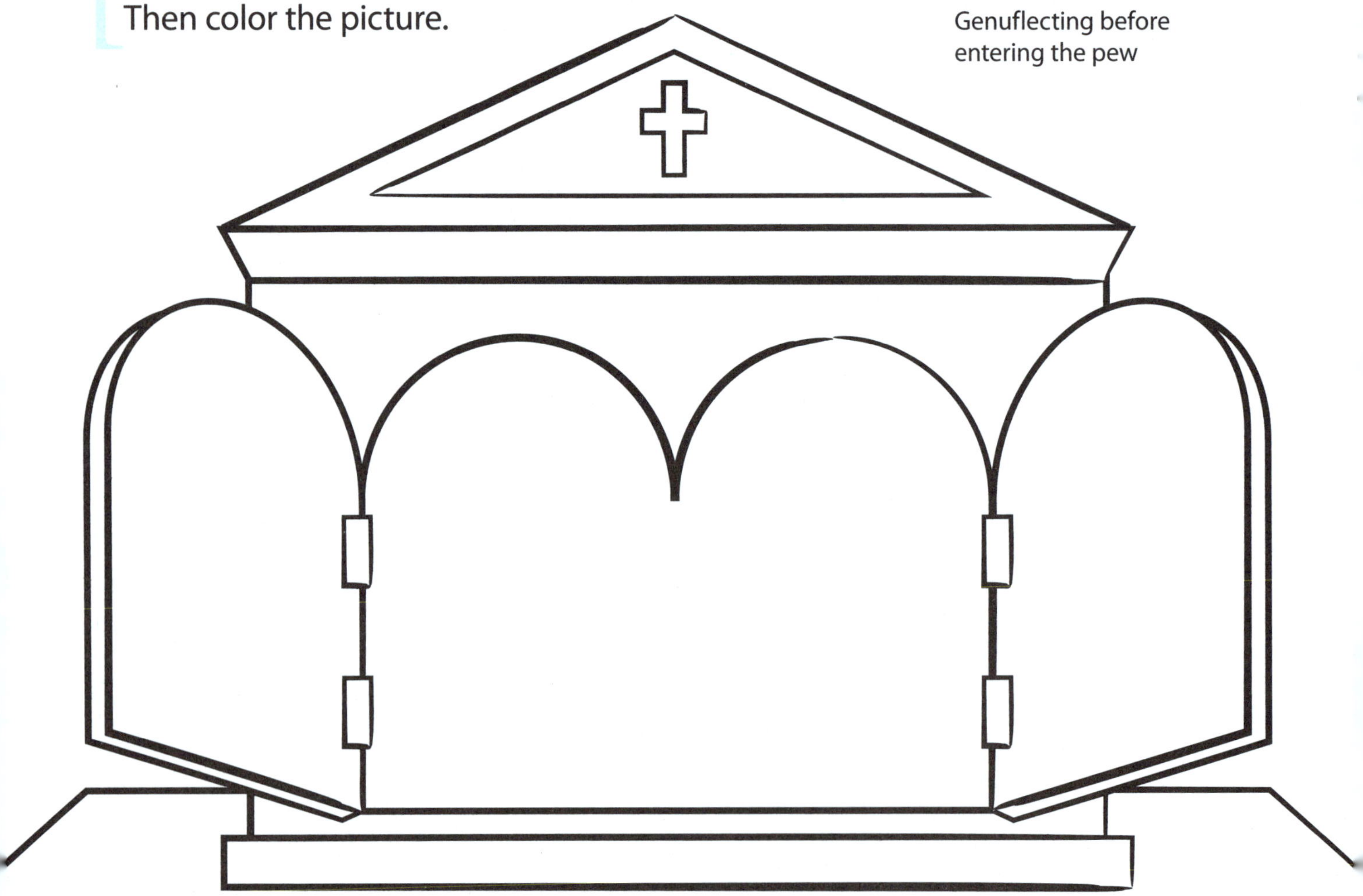

Living My Faith

Faith Summary

We go to Mass every Sunday. We share a special meal. The bread and wine become the Body and Blood of Jesus Christ. Jesus is with us in his Body and Blood.

Words I Learned

Blessed Sacrament **Eucharist**
consecration **Last Supper**

Ways of Being Like Jesus

Jesus gave thanks to his Father at the Last Supper. *Pray before and after meals. Thank God for all his blessings.*

Prayer

Jesus, help me remember what you did for me.

ACTIVITY: Sacrament of the Eucharist

Finish each sentence with the correct word from the word box.

Mass	**Life**	**Supper**

1. Jesus is the Bread of ______________________.
2. The meal Jesus shared is called the Last ____________.
3. Jesus is with us in his Body and Blood at ____________.

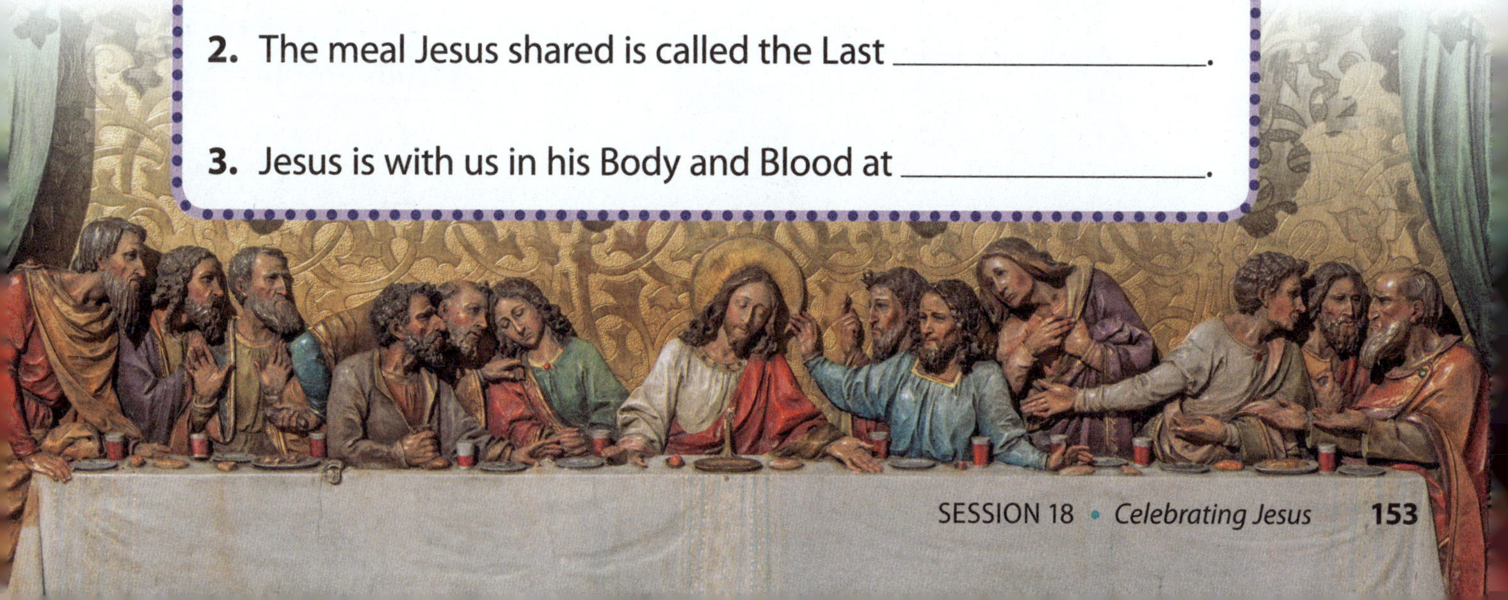

With My Family

Scripture Together

Before Jesus died, he shared a meal with his friends. We call this meal the Last Supper. Our most holy celebration of the Mass comes during Holy Communion. When we share the consecrated bread and wine, we receive the Body and Blood of Jesus.

As a family, read about the Last Supper in Mark 14:22–25. When you have finished, discuss the Scripture. You may use the following questions to prompt discussion:

- What did Jesus say when he broke the bread?
- What might you have said to Jesus at the Last Supper?
- How is Jesus' Last Supper like our celebration of the Mass?

Family Prayer

Pray together:
Dear God, thank you for the food you give us. Help us remember that you are with us. Amen.

Faith on the Go

Ask one another: *What's your favorite part of the Mass? Why?*

ACTIVITY: Family Meal

Work together to plan a special meal. Have all family members participate. Pray a blessing before and after the meal thanking God for food and family.

Listening to Our Father

SESSION 19

GOD'S WORD

Read and listen to Matthew 6:5–8.

Evening Prayer, John Bagnold Burgess, 19th century

God the Father loves us very much. He wants to be close to us. His Son, Jesus, tells us how to be close to the Father. Jesus teaches us how to pray.

We do not pray to impress others. We pray to grow closer to God. We talk to God. We praise him. We thank God for loving us. We ask him to help us. We trust him.

God always hears our prayers. We also listen for God when we pray. We hear God's Word in the Bible. We think about what God tells us. We try to live as God wants us to live. We try to live as God's children.

Prayer

Dear God, help me listen for you when I pray. Help me understand what you are telling me.

EXPLORE

Elijah Listens for God

This Bible story is told in the first Book of Kings. Elijah loved God. He wanted to be alone with God. Elijah went into a cave. God told him to go outside. God said he would pass by. He told Elijah to listen for him.

Whoosh! A great wind blew. But Elijah could not hear God. Roar! A loud earthquake shook the ground. Elijah could not hear God. Hiss! A fire lit up the sky. Elijah still could not hear God.

Elijah stood very still. Then he heard something. It was a tiny whisper. He listened closely. It was God talking to him.

Reading God's Word

Everyone who listens to my Father and learns from him comes to me.

John 6:45

The Holy Spirit Guides Us

We talk to God when we pray. We listen closely. God's grace helps us hear him. God's grace comes to us in the sacraments.

In Baptism the Holy Spirit gives us grace. Baptism gives us new life. In the Sacrament of **Confirmation,** the Holy Spirit gives us more grace. Confirmation makes our faith stronger. It helps us hear God the Father. The Holy Spirit helps us do what God asks us to do.

ACTIVITY: The Sacrament of Confirmation

Complete each sentence. Write the correct word from the word box.

Baptism	Confirmation	grace	Holy Spirit	pray

We talk and listen to God when we ____________________.

The Holy Spirit gives us God's ____________________.

____________________ gives us new life in God.

____________________ makes our faith in God stronger.

The ____________________ helps us do what God asks.

ART PRINT 19

Art Print 19 shows three women singing and dancing. How and when do you pray?

Praying to God

What do we tell God?
We tell him we are happy.
We tell him we are sad.
We can tell God anything!

How do we pray?
We use words.
We sing songs.
We use **gestures.**
We dance.
We listen to God.

Where can we pray?
We can pray at home.
We can pray at school.
We can pray in the car.
We can pray at church.
We can pray anywhere!

ACTIVITY: How I Pray

Draw a picture of yourself praying.

Link to Liturgy

We can pray anytime and anywhere. We can pray about anything. We pray together at Mass.

Listen for God

Elijah wanted to hear God. Loud sounds filled the air. Elijah listened closely. Then he heard a small sound. It was God talking to him.

Listen for God as Elijah did. Pray the prayer below.

Prayer

Think about the sounds you hear around you. Block out the loud sounds. Listen to the soft sounds. Do you hear rain? Rustling leaves? Soft whispers?

Now, be very quiet, as Elijah was. Listen for God. He is all around you. Tell God you will always listen. Tell God you will hear what he wants you to know.

Where Can We Find God?

God is always with us. He is everywhere. God wants us to talk to him. He wants us to listen to him. We will hear God if we listen closely. We will hear God if we focus our thoughts. This is what Elijah did.

ACTIVITY: Places to Pray

Where do you like to pray? Draw a picture of it. Then answer the questions.

What do you want to say to God or ask him?

____

____

What do you think God is saying to you?

____

____

Living My Faith

Faith Summary

God is everywhere. We can pray to him anywhere. We may need to listen closely to hear him.

Words I Learned

Confirmation **gestures**

Ways of Being Like Jesus

Jesus listened to God his Father. *Find a quiet time each day to listen to God in your heart.*

Prayer

Dear God, you are always in my heart.

ACTIVITY: God Talks to Us

God wants us to be close to him.

Trace the letters. Color the words. Then read the sentence.

God is always with us.

With My Family

Scripture Together

Jesus is our best teacher. He calls us to listen and learn from him so that we may know God the Father. We learn from Jesus how to pray. We learn how to praise God the Father.

As a family, read about Jesus' joy and gratitude for the gift of the Father's showing himself to us in Matthew 11:25–27. When you have finished, discuss the Scripture. You may use the following questions to prompt discussion:

- To whom does Jesus say God has revealed himself?
- How do you show your joy and gratitude to God?
- How can you and our family learn more about Jesus?

Family Prayer

Pray together:
Dear God, thank you for teaching us to listen for you. We know you are always with us. Amen.

Faith on the Go

Ask one another: *Where is your favorite place to go when you want to pray?*

ACTIVITY: Prayer Space

Designate a place in or around your home as a prayer space. Spend time there each day talking and listening to God.

Celebrating Lent and Holy Week

SESSION 20

GOD'S WORD

Read and listen to Matthew 4:1–2.

Jesus being led into the wilderness to be tempted by the devil, William Brassey Hole, 1905

Jesus went into the desert alone. He prayed for 40 days. He prepared his heart. He got ready to do his Father's work.

In the Bible, the number 40 is important. Many people get ready for 40 days. Some people get ready for 40 years. They prepare. Something important will happen.

The season of Lent lasts for 40 days. During Lent, we prepare our hearts. We pray to God. We try harder to follow Jesus' example. Something important will happen soon.

Prayer

Dear Jesus, help me grow closer to you this Lent.

EXPLORE

Growing Closer to God

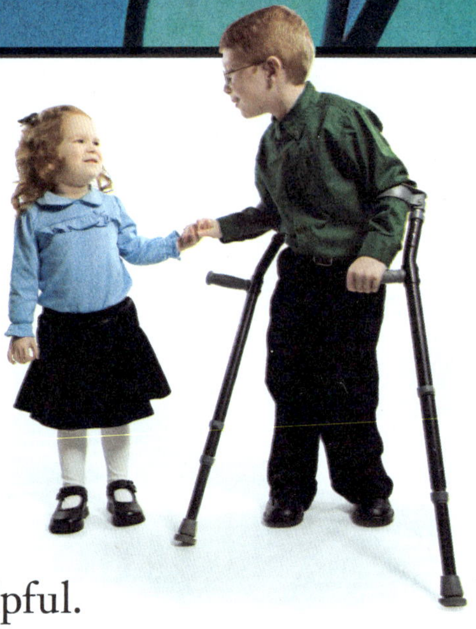

During **Lent,** we prepare to celebrate at Easter. Jesus rose from the dead at Easter. Lent is a time to grow closer to God.

We think about how Jesus lived. We try to be more like Jesus. We pray. We make up for things we have done wrong. We are kind and helpful.

The Lenten season begins on Ash Wednesday. The season lasts for 40 days. The last week of Lent is **Holy Week.** We recall Jesus' suffering, Death, and Resurrection. We also pray for others during Holy Week.

ACTIVITY: Ash Wednesday

On Ash Wednesday, a priest, a deacon, or a lay minister makes the Sign of the Cross in ashes on our forehead. Finish the prayer. Write the correct word or words from the word box.

Father	**Holy Spirit**	**Son**

In the name of the ______________________________

and of the ______________________________

and of the ______________________________.

Reading God's Word

Children, let us love not in word or speech but in deed and truth.

1 John 3:18

Mass During Lent and Holy Week

The **Alleluia** is a joyful song of praise to God. We usually sing it before the gospel reading. During Lent and Holy Week, we do not sing the Alleluia. We hear music or sing other words.

What We Experience

You may see plain linens in church. The decorations are simple. The priest's vestments are a violet color. You will not see flowers around the altar.

ACTIVITY: My Parish Priest

Write your priest's name below. Then color the Lenten vestments.

Father ____.

Did You Know?

Ashes are made by burning last year's blessed palm branches.

ART PRINT 20

Art Print 20 shows Jesus on the Cross.
How will you prepare your heart during Lent?

Celebrating Lent and Holy Week

Jesus always prayed. He prayed to God, his Father. Jesus grew closer to his Father. As Christians, we pray to God the Father too. Jesus teaches us how to be closer to God the Father.

- Jesus cared for those who were poor and sick.
- Jesus prayed.
- Jesus shared God's message with others.

The season of Lent reminds us to live as Jesus did. Each time we make a choice to be like Jesus, we grow closer to God.

ACTIVITY: Grow Closer to God

Write a prayer to God the Father. Ask him to help you always do your best. Tell him you will be more like Jesus, his Son, during Lent.

Living My Faith

Faith Summary

During Lent and Holy Week, we try to be more like Jesus. It is a time for us to grow closer to God.

Words I Learned

Alleluia   Holy Week   Lent

Ways of Being Like Jesus

Jesus loved others and showed kindness. *Speak kind words. Be more patient.*

Prayer

Dear God, help me listen to you every day, especially during Lent.

ACTIVITY: Lent Crossword Puzzle

Use the clues to fill in this puzzle.

Lent   violet   seven

Across

3. The _____ days before Easter are called Holy Week.

Down

1. The color of the priest's vestments is _____.
2. _____ lasts 40 days.

With My Family

Scripture Together

Jesus taught and helped many people. Crowds followed him from place to place. Their needs were great. While Jesus willingly welcomed everyone, there were times when he needed to be alone to rest and to pray.

As a family, read about Jesus' practice of prayer in **Luke 5:15–16**. When you have finished, discuss the Scripture. You may use the following questions to prompt discussion:

- Where did Jesus go to pray?
- Where do you go to be alone?
- How can you help our family make time to rest and pray?

Family Prayer

Pray together:
Dear God, be with us as we enjoy this season. Thank you for the gift of your Son, Jesus. Amen.

Faith on the Go

Ask one another: *How can I love and serve others as Jesus did?*

ACTIVITY: Reflection Journals

Participate in special prayer experiences of the season, such as the Stations of the Cross and the services of Holy Week. After each, have family members make a journal entry or draw a picture to reflect.

UNIT 5

Morality, Our Lived Faith

UNIT 5

Morality, Our Lived Faith

Saint Ignatius of Loyola

SPAIN

Ignatius was born long ago. He was a brave soldier. However, he did not think of God often.

One day Ignatius was in a battle. He was hit by a cannonball and hurt. As he healed, he read two books. One book was about Jesus' life. The other book was about the saints' lives.

Ignatius began to change. He started to pray. He thought more about God. Ignatius decided to live like Jesus. He obeyed God the Father's rules. He cared for others. He loved his family and God's world.

Ignatius loved God above all. Ignatius studied and wrote. He taught many others about God. He was one of God's greatest followers.

Be Inspired

May I love the Lord more and follow him more closely.

Saint Ignatius of Loyola

God in Everything

Ignatius found God in all people and all things. He did his best to share God's love. He taught others to use all their senses to get closer to God. Ignatius taught others to think about their actions. He helped them make good choices.

Reading God's Word

Teach me to do your will,
for you are my God.
May your kind spirit guide me.

Psalm 143:10

Ignatius taught people to think carefully about their day. He taught them to be thankful.

ACTIVITY: I Am Thankful

Think about your day so far. Write four things for which you are thankful. Circle one thing from your list. Spend a few moments thinking about it. Then pray to God to thank him.

I am thankful for

1. ______________________________

____

2. ______________________________

____

3. ______________________________

____

4. ______________________________

____

Making Good Decisions

SESSION 21

GOD'S WORD

Read and listen to Matthew 7:24–27.

A house built on rock by the sea

We can learn from Jesus' stories. They teach us how to live. They teach us how to grow closer to God the Father.

Jesus spoke to the people. They knew how to build a strong house. A house built on a solid base will stand strong in storms.

Prayer

Jesus, help me follow your teachings, so I may find my way to God the Father.

Like a house, we need a solid base to build a good life. People who listen to Jesus have a solid base. Jesus' teachings help us make good choices. Jesus' teachings help us find our way to God the Father.

EXPLORE

God's Rules

God the Father gives us rules because he loves us. We call God's rules his **commandments.** They show us how to live as children of God.

God gave us these **Ten Commandments.**

1. I am your God; love nothing more than me.
2. Use God's name with respect.
3. Keep the Lord's Day holy.
4. Honor and obey your parents.
5. Treat all human life with respect.
6. Respect married life.
7. Respect what belongs to others.
8. Tell the truth.
9. Honor the family relationships of your neighbors and friends.
10. Be happy with what you have.

Decisions

You make decisions, or choices, every day. It is not always easy to choose right over wrong. Think about God's commandments. They help us make good decisions. God will always help us follow his rules.

ACTIVITY: God's Commandments

Draw a line to match each commandment with a decision. Circle the good decisions.

Commandment	Decision
Honor and obey your parents.	You decide to take time to talk to God.
I am your God; love nothing more than me.	You decide to listen when Mom says it is time for bed.
Tell the truth.	You decide to keep a hat that you find at school.
Respect what belongs to others.	You decide to make up a story when you break a vase.

Did You Know?

The Ten Commandments are fulfilled in Jesus' Great Commandment. The Great Commandment tells us to love God and our neighbor. There is no commandment greater than this.

ART PRINT 21

Art Print 21 shows a woman serving food to people in need. She has made a good decision. What helps you make good decisions?

Good Decisions

How can we make good decisions? We can ask three questions.

ACTIVITY: My Big Decision

Write about a good decision you made. Why was it a good decision?

Reading God's Word

"You shall love the Lord, your God, with all your heart, with all your soul, and with all your mind. This is the greatest and the first commandment. The second is like it: You shall love your neighbor as yourself."

Matthew 22:37–39

Begin Each Day with Prayer

We have new decisions to make each day. God will always help you make good decisions. Now, pray the prayer below.

Prayer

Think about the commandments God gave us. Talk with God. Ask him to help you do what is right. Ask him to help you be kind.

Start each day by talking with God. We can pray the Morning Prayer.

Morning Prayer

God, our Father, I offer you today
all that I think and do and say.
I offer it with what was done on earth
by Jesus Christ, your Son.

Make Good Decisions

The Ten Commandments show us how to love both God and other people. Think about the commandments. They can help you make good choices.

ACTIVITY: What Should You Do?

Read each group of sentences. For a good decision, draw a  .
For a bad decision, draw a  .

Dad asks you to pick up your toys. You do it right away.

You find some money. It is not yours. You take it anyway.

You did not do your homework. Your teacher asks you about it. You tell the truth.

Living My Faith

Faith Summary

God gave us commandments. They help us make good decisions. Good decisions bring us peace.

Words I Learned

commandment **Ten Commandments**

Ways of Being Like Jesus

Jesus always did what was right. *Treat others as you would like to be treated.*

Prayer

Jesus, my friend, thank you for helping me follow God's rules. I will try to make good decisions.

ACTIVITY: My Foundation

God's commandments help us build a good life. On the stone tablet, write one good decision you can make today.

AT HOME

With My Family

Scripture Together

Often the people who heard Jesus teach asked him questions. In Luke 10:25–28, Jesus tells the scholar to think about a law he already knows. Jesus reminds the man that knowing the law is not enough. We must act to truly follow God's rules and grow closer to him.

As a family, read about the Greatest Commandment in **Luke 10:25–28**. When you have finished, discuss the Scripture. You may use the following questions to prompt discussion:

- What answer does the man in the story give to Jesus?
- Why do you think Jesus answers the man's question with another question?
- How can you show your love for God through how you act toward your neighbor?

Family Prayer

Pray together:
Dear God, thank you for giving us your commandments. Help us always follow them. Amen.

Faith on the Go

Ask one another: *What's your favorite way to show your love to someone?*

ACTIVITY: Love of Neighbor

Show your love for your neighbors. Surprise them with flowers or a kind note.

Jesus Cares for Us

SESSION 22

GOD'S WORD

Read and listen to Luke 15:8–10.

Parable of the lost coin

Jesus tells stories to teach us. He told a story to help people understand God the Father's love for them.

Many of us have lost something. Like the woman in the story, we search and search for it. If we find it, we are overjoyed. We feel complete.

God searches for us when we lose our way to him. We move away from God when we make bad decisions. If we ask, God will forgive us. We will feel God the Father's and Jesus the Son's loving care. The Holy Spirit will guide us. We will not feel lost anymore.

Prayer

God the Father, help me feel your loving care.

EXPLORE

God Always Forgives

When we choose to do something wrong, we **sin.** We hurt our friendships with God and other people.

A sin can be something we do. A sin can be something we say.

ACTIVITY: Avoid Sin

Read each idea that describes how someone might sin. Then write how you can avoid the sin.

Instead of taking a toy that's not mine,

I can ______________________________

______________________________.

Instead of telling a lie, I can ____________

____

______________________________.

Forgiveness Gives Us Peace

When we are sorry, we ask God for **forgiveness.** God always forgives us. God's love is greater than any sin. Forgiveness gives us peace.

We can forgive others the way God forgives us. When people tell us they are sorry, we can forgive them. It makes us feel less sad or angry. We can show that we care for them. Forgiving and caring for others helps us grow closer to God.

Sometimes we sin and hurt someone else. We can say we are sorry. Then that person can forgive us.

There are many ways to say we are sorry.

Link to Liturgy

After the Greeting at the beginning of Mass, we ask Jesus for forgiveness.

ART PRINT

22

Art Print 22 shows Jesus as the Good Shepherd. What can you do when you have turned away from God and are lost?

The Good Shepherd

According to the Gospel of Luke, Jesus told this story:

Imagine you are a shepherd. You have 100 sheep. One gets lost. You leave all your sheep to look for the lost one.

You look everywhere. Then you finally find it. You are so happy!

You carry the sheep home carefully. You tell everyone that you found your lost sheep.

A person who does something wrong is like that lost sheep. All of heaven is happy when that lost sheep is found.

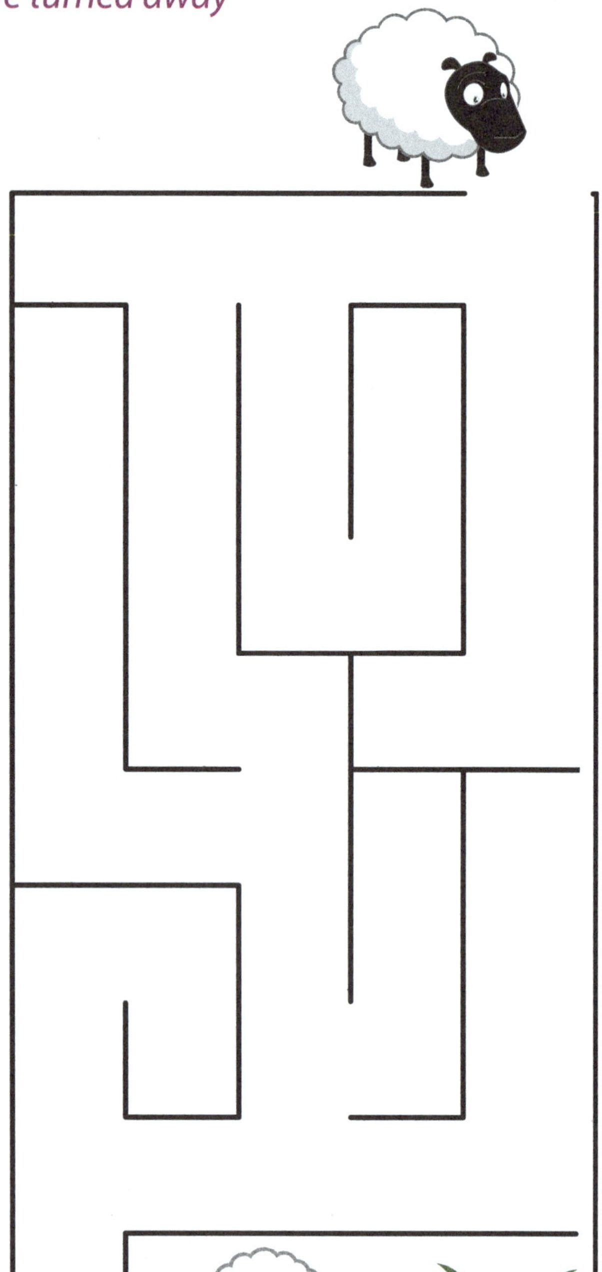

ACTIVITY: Show Me the Way

Draw the correct path through the maze to help the lost sheep get home.

Pray for Forgiveness

Think about the story of the lost sheep. Imagine being that lost sheep. Now pray the prayer below.

Prayer

How do you feel? Lonely? Scared? Now, imagine a shepherd coming to find you. Think about how happy and safe you feel.

This is how Jesus cares for us. Sometimes we do things that we know are unkind or wrong. Jesus is always with us. He forgives us.

Think about a time you did something that you knew was wrong. Tell Jesus you are sorry. Ask him to forgive you. Listen for what Jesus wants you to know. Jesus will always love you, no matter what.

A Caring Shepherd

Jesus is like a caring shepherd. He always brings us back to him. He does so as gently as a shepherd carries a little lamb.

ACTIVITY: Our Good Shepherd

Write the correct word from the word box to complete each sentence.

lost	**shepherd**	**finds**	**sheep**

Jesus is like a ______________________.

We are like his ______________________.

Jesus looks for us when we are ______________________.

He always ______________________ us.

Reading God's Word

Jesus said, "I am the good shepherd."

John 10:11

Living My Faith

Faith Summary

God's love is greater than any sin. When we have done something bad, we say we are sorry. God always forgives us.

Words I Learned

forgiveness **sin**

Ways of Being Like Jesus

Jesus taught us about forgiveness. *When someone says "I'm sorry," show them you care. Say "I forgive you."*

Prayer

Jesus, thank you for teaching me about forgiveness. Help me forgive others.

ACTIVITY: Forgiving Words

What do we say for forgiveness? Trace each word. Then read the sentences.

I'm sorry.

I forgive you.

With My Family

Scripture Together

After Jesus' Death and Resurrection, crowds of people came to be near the Apostles. Like Jesus, the Apostles cared for the people. In Jesus' name, they healed and made believers of them.

As a family, read about the Apostles' signs and wonders in Acts of the Apostles 5:12–16. When you have finished, discuss the Scripture. You may use the following questions to prompt discussion:

- Why did people carry the sick into the streets?
- If you were there, would you have gone to be near the Apostles? Why or why not?
- How does this story show that Jesus loves and cares for you?

Family Prayer

Pray together:
Dear God, help us show our love for others by forgiving them as you always forgive us. Amen.

Faith on the Go

Ask one another: *How can we care for someone who has hurt us?*

ACTIVITY: How to Forgive

Write the letters *F, O, R, G, I, V, E* on slips of paper and work together to unscramble the letters. Then take turns completing this sentence: "I am like Jesus when I _______." Possible answers include "say I'm sorry," "forgive others," "pray to God for help," "show that I care," and "receive the grace to overcome bad feelings."

Jesus Loves Families

SESSION 23

GOD'S WORD

Read and listen to Ephesians 6:1–4.

Parents and their children

Paul was a leader in the early Church. He wrote many letters. Many of his letters are in the Bible.

Paul's letters help us understand Jesus' teachings. His letters help us follow God the Father's rules. God's rules are called commandments.

God wants us to respect our parents. God wants our parents to show love for their children. We show God's love by loving our families.

Prayer

Jesus, Son of God, help me love my parents and do what they ask.

Jesus Obeyed His Parents

The Gospel according to Luke tells us this story. Jesus and his parents were away from home. They were at a great celebration with family and friends. On the way home, Mary and Joseph could not find Jesus. He was not with family or friends. No one had seen Jesus. Mary and Joseph were very worried. They rushed back.

They looked and looked for Jesus. Finally, they found him in the Temple. He was listening to the teachers. He was asking questions. Mary said to Jesus, "We have been so worried about you."

Jesus went home with his parents. He was obedient to them.

A Gift from God

God gave your parents a gift. He gave them YOU.

Your parents love and care for you. They want you to be safe. They want you to learn about God.

God wants you to **honor,** or respect, your parents. He wants you to thank them for all they do for you. You honor and thank your parents when you **obey** them, or do what they ask you to do.

ACTIVITY: Obey Your Parents

Why do we obey our parents? Mark an X next to each reason.

- They want what is best for me.
- They take care of me.
- God wants me to respect them.
- They give me good gifts.
- They teach me right from wrong.

ART PRINT 23

Art Print 23 shows a family spending time together at a park. How do you like to spend time with your family?

God and Family

Your parents have loved you since before you were born. They want you to be healthy. They want you to be happy. They want the very best for you.

When you listen to your parents, God is happy. When you do what your parents ask you to do, God is happy. When you love your parents, God is happy.

ACTIVITY: I Love My Family

Draw a picture that shows one way you can love your parents.

Did You Know?

"Honor and obey your parents" is a commandment. Jesus followed this commandment.

A Prayer to End Each Day

At the end of each day, we think about what we have done. We think about the decisions we made. We think about how we showed God our love.

End each day by talking with God. We can pray the Evening Prayer below.

Prayer

As you pray the prayer, think about your family. Think about how you showed them your love. Ask God to bless them.

Evening Prayer

God, our Father, this day is done.
We ask you and Jesus Christ, your Son,
that with the Spirit, our welcome guest,
you guard our sleep and bless our rest.

Show You Care

Your parents love you and care for you. God wants you to show that you love and care for your parents too.

ACTIVITY: Love and Care

Find and circle the words shown in the word box.

honor	love	obey	help

Z	L	Q	P	L	V
H	O	N	O	R	Z
W	V	Q	B	R	I
X	E	H	E	L	P
K	I	B	Y	Q	W

Reading God's Word

Honor your father and your mother, that you may have a long life in the land the LORD your God is giving you.

Exodus 20:12

Living My Faith

Faith Summary

Jesus loved and obeyed his parents. God wants us to obey our parents too. When we show love for our parents, we show love for God.

Prayer

Jesus, thank you for teaching me to obey and care for my parents.

Words I Learned

honor **obey**

Ways of Being Like Jesus

Jesus honored his parents. *Show your parents that you love and honor them. Obey them and be polite. Thank them for all they do.*

ACTIVITY: Family Love

Write how you honor your parents. Then draw yourself showing love and care for your parents.

I honor my parents when I ______________________________

____.

With My Family

Scripture Together

As loving parents, Mary and Joseph cared for Jesus. Following the laws of their faith, they took the child Jesus to the Temple to give an offering to God. There they met a holy man named Simeon, who embraced Jesus and thanked God for letting him see Jesus.

As a family, read about the Presentation in the Temple in **Luke 2:22–35**. When you have finished, discuss the Scripture. You may use the following questions to prompt discussion:

- Why did Mary and Joseph bring Jesus to the Temple?
- How might you have reacted if you had seen Jesus in the Temple?
- How can you thank God for giving our family the gift of his Son, Jesus?

Family Prayer

Pray together:
Dear God, thank you for the gift of our family. Help us better listen to and love one another each day. Amen.

Faith on the Go

Ask one another: *What is the easiest family rule for you to follow? What is the hardest rule?*

ACTIVITY: Home Night

Plan a family home night in which the family stays home to spend time together. Plan one or more activities, such as prayer or Scripture study, music, games, and treats, that will strengthen your relationships with one another.

God Loves the World

SESSION 24

GOD'S WORD

Read and listen to Daniel 3:72–81.

God Created the Earth and Continues to Care for It, Elizabeth Wang, 2004

God the Father blessed us with a beautiful world. We have everything we need to live and grow. God wants us to care for our world. We can show our thanks to God in prayer.

Think of every little thing that makes up the world. Think of every blade of grass. Think of every bird. Think of every drop of rain and ray of sun. Everything in the world is a gift from God. We praise God for his many wonderful gifts.

Prayer

God, help me take care of your world.

Caring for Our World

God made our world. That is why it is beautiful. We help keep it beautiful. We take care of the animals and plants. We do this for God. We do this for ourselves. We do this for our **neighbors.** As Christians, we believe all people are our neighbors. God made every person in his image. Every person deserves our care and respect. All of God's creation deserves our care and respect.

Did You Know?

Forests are important places. They give animals homes. They keep our air clean. They even give us important medicines.

Caring for God's Creatures

All animals, even wild ones, are God's creatures. God wants us to care for all of his creation.

ACTIVITY: How Do We Care?

Read the story and the two endings. Circle the ending that shows how to care for God's creatures.

Matt and Kara were playing by a pond when Matt saw something move. "What is it?" asked Matt. It was a small turtle. Matt and Kara called to Mom and Dad. "Look what we found. May we keep it?"

ENDING 1

"Sure," they replied. "This pond is home to many turtles. We can take this turtle."

ENDING 2

"No," they replied. "God made this pond. It is this turtle's home. We have to care for God's beautiful world."

ART PRINT 24

Art Print 24 shows the Garden of Eden from the Bible. Why is it important to take care of God's world?

The First Garden

God took the first man to a beautiful garden. He asked the man to take care of it. Then God created different animals and birds. God told the man to give them names.

> The man gave names to all the tame animals, all the birds of the air, and all the wild animals. *Genesis 2:20*

ACTIVITY: I Care for God's Creation

Find Adam and Eve in the picture below and circle them. Then write about your favorite thing in God's creation.

____

____

Reading God's Word

The earth has yielded its harvest.

Psalm 67:7

A Nature Prayer

God loves us. He fills our lives with beautiful things.

Now, pray the prayer below.

Prayer

Imagine you are outside. You feel a gentle breeze. It is your favorite kind of day. Look around. Do you see your favorite flowers and trees? Do you see your favorite animals? Imagine you see all your favorite things. God created these things for you.

Thank God for all your favorite things. Tell him how you will care for them. Listen in your heart to what God wants you to know.

What Can You Do?

We can show God how much we love him. We can care for God's world. We can care for the earth. We can care for the animals and plants. We can care for our neighbors. How will you care for God's world?

ACTIVITY: I Can Do It

Choose to care for the earth, an animal, a plant, or another person. Finish the sentence in the box. Then draw a picture of how you will care for it.

I can care for ______________________________.

Link to Liturgy

At the end of Mass, we go in peace to show our love for God and all of creation.

Living My Faith

Faith Summary

God made a beautiful world. He wants us to care for plants and animals. We take care of them for ourselves and others.

Word I Learned

neighbor

Ways of Being Like Jesus

Jesus cared for the gifts his Father gave him. *Care for God the Father's world. Be kind to every living thing.*

Prayer

God our Father, everything you create is good. I will care for your creation.

ACTIVITY: My Prayer of Praise

Write a prayer of praise. Think of three things you want to praise God for creating. Write one on each line.

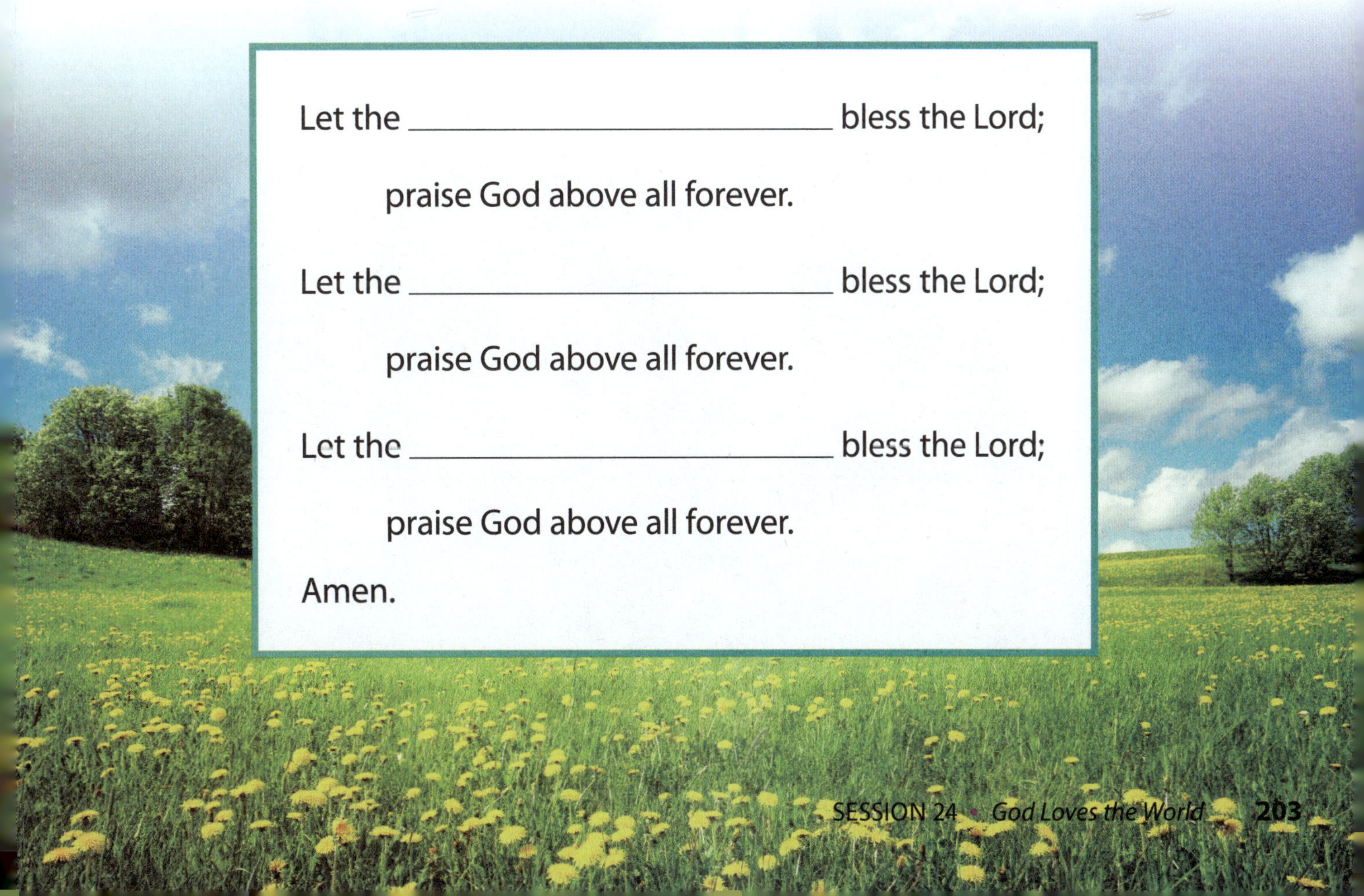

Let the ______________________ bless the Lord;

praise God above all forever.

Let the ______________________ bless the Lord;

praise God above all forever.

Let the ______________________ bless the Lord;

praise God above all forever.

Amen.

With My Family

Scripture Together

We can give praise and glory to God in song. A hymn is a song that urges people to joyfully sing out praise to God.

As a family, enjoy a hymn that praises God's marvelous deeds by reading **Psalm 98**. When you have finished, discuss the Scripture. You may use the following questions to prompt discussion:

- According to the psalm, what should all the earth do?
- In what way, such as through prayerful song or actions, do you like to praise God? Why?
- What do you picture in your mind when you hear Psalm 98?

Family Prayer

Pray together:
Dear God, we are grateful for this beautiful world. Help us protect all you've created. Amen.

Faith on the Go

Ask one another: *What one thing can you do every day to care for our world?*

ACTIVITY: Care for God's Creation

Talk about ways to care for God's creation around you, such as making your porch or yard animal friendly. Choose one way and work together to complete it.

Celebrating Easter

SESSION 25

GOD'S WORD

Read and listen to Luke 24:1–8.

Jesus died on the Cross and was buried in a tomb. Three days later some friends went to his tomb. Jesus was gone. Jesus had risen.

The Resurrection of Jesus

We celebrate Jesus' Resurrection on Easter. We rejoice. Jesus died and rose from the dead. He saved us. He gave us new life. We praise God the Father during the Easter season. We thank him for sending his Son, Jesus, to save us.

Easter is the beginning of a new season of grace. Jesus is with us. We celebrate the feasts of the season together at Mass. We remember what Jesus has done for us. The Church celebrates for 50 days!

Prayer

Thank you, Jesus. We celebrate your glorious Resurrection.

We Celebrate During Easter

We celebrate **Easter** on the Sunday after the first full moon of spring. The Easter season begins with the Easter Vigil on Holy Saturday evening. The Easter season continues for the next 50 days.

Easter is the most important Christian feast. It is the time when we celebrate Jesus Christ's Resurrection. Jesus died on the Cross for us. God the Father raised his Son, Jesus, from the dead. We are glad because Jesus saves us all.

Reading God's Word

[Jesus] stood in their midst and said to them, "Peace be with you."

Luke 24:36

ACTIVITY: Praise Be to God

Use the key to color the picture below. Then read the word of praise.

1 – blue 2 – green 3 – pink 4 – yellow

Mass During Easter

We are joyful during the Easter season. At Mass on Easter, we joyfully sing and pray the Alleluia, a prayer of praise to God the Father. We are happy because his Son, Jesus, saves us all.

What We Experience

When you look around your church, you may see symbols of Easter. Notice the priest's vestments and altar linens. They are white as a symbol of Jesus' Resurrection. Other symbols are the paschal candle and Easter lily. The paschal candle and white lilies are symbols of new life.

ACTIVITY: The Easter Lily

Color the lily. Then think of someone you will pray for this Easter season. Write the name on the line.

I will pray for ______________________.

Did You Know?

The Church celebrates the day of Jesus' Resurrection on the "eighth day," Sunday, which is called the Lord's Day.

ART PRINT 25

Art Print 25 shows the risen Jesus Christ and the women who went to the tomb Easter morning. How do you celebrate Easter?

Celebrating Easter

After Jesus died on the Cross, he was laid in a tomb. Two women went to the tomb to honor him. They saw that Jesus' body was gone. But Jesus appeared to them and told them not to be afraid. The women were so happy.

On Easter we celebrate Jesus' rising from the dead. We sing and pray "Alleluia!"

ACTIVITY: We Meet Jesus

Connect the dots to see where and with whom you can meet Jesus.

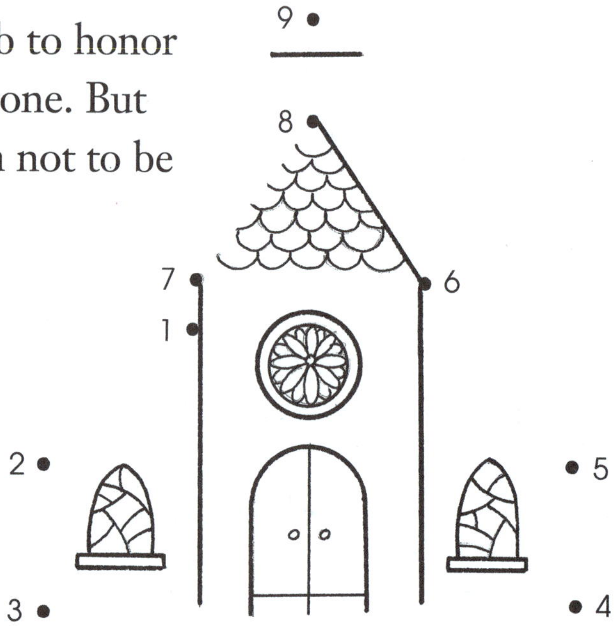

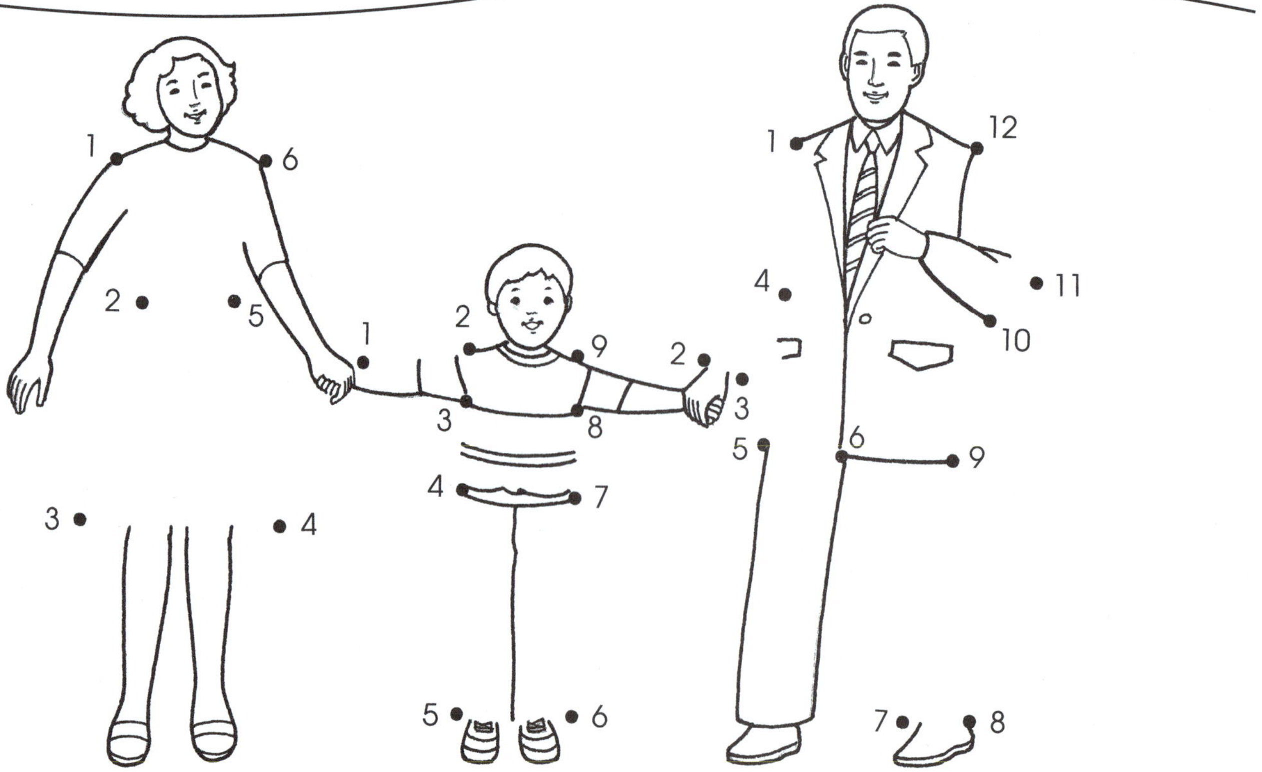

Living My Faith

Faith Summary

At Easter, we celebrate Jesus' Resurrection. God the Father raised his Son, Jesus, from the dead to save us from sin and death.

Word I Learned

Easter

Ways of Being Like Jesus

Jesus gave us the gift of himself. *Give of yourself to others. Share a song, a dance, or something you made.*

Prayer

Dear Jesus, you fill my heart with joy and love.

ACTIVITY: Share the Good News

When we are excited about something, we share news about it. Share the news about Jesus' Resurrection. Finish each sentence. Use the words from the word box.

Cross	life	rose	saved

Good News!

Jesus died on the ______________.

He ______________ from the dead for us.

Jesus ______________ us.

He gave us new ______________.

With My Family

Scripture Together

After his Resurrection, Jesus appeared to his disciples. He explained why he died on the Cross and rose from the dead. He told them to go out and tell people of all nations about him.

Family Prayer

Pray together:
Dear God, may your love be resurrected in our hearts during this Easter season. Amen.

As a family, read about Jesus' appearance to the disciples in **Luke 24:36–49**. When you have finished, discuss the Scripture. You may use the following questions to prompt discussion:

- What was the first thing Jesus said to the disciples?
- If you were there when Jesus appeared, what would you have thought?
- How can you share Jesus' peace with others?

Faith on the Go

Ask one another: *How will you celebrate Jesus' Resurrection at Easter?*

ACTIVITY: Scavenger Hunt

Go on a scavenger hunt in the church. Look for and discuss the meaning of symbols of new life such as light, a candle, water, the word *Alleluia*, a cross, a lamb, a rabbit, an Easter lily, a butterfly, and an egg.

The Year in Our Church

Liturgical Calendar

The liturgical calendar shows us the feasts and seasons of the Church year.

Liturgical Year

- During the **Advent** season, we get ready to welcome Jesus.

- The **Christmas** season celebrates the time when Jesus was born.
- The season of **Lent** is the time before Easter.

- **Holy Week** is the week before Easter. We remember that Jesus died for us.
- On **Easter,** Jesus rose from the dead. During the Easter season, we joyfully celebrate for 50 days.
- **Ordinary Time** is a season set aside for everyday living. We grow as followers of Jesus.

We celebrate many feast days, such as Pentecost and All Saints Day, within the seasons:

- On **Pentecost** the Holy Spirit came to Jesus' friends.
- **All Saints Day** is the day on which we remember everyone in heaven.

Advent

Mary and Joseph waited for Jesus to be born. We wait to celebrate Jesus' birth. We call this time of waiting the Advent season.

Prayer

God the Father, help me be patient as I prepare for Jesus' birth at Christmas.

Waiting for Jesus

Jesus was about to be born. Mary and Joseph were getting ready for him. At that same time, their ruler wanted to count all his people. Joseph had to go far from home to Bethlehem to be counted. Mary had to go too.

> While they were there, the time came for her to have her child.
>
> *Luke 2:6*

They had nowhere to rest. So they stayed in a stable. They waited there for Jesus to be born.

ACTIVITY: What Did Mary and Joseph Do?

Unscramble the letters. Then write them in the blanks.

w t a i d e

Mary and Joseph

____ ____ ____ ____ ____ ____

for Jesus.

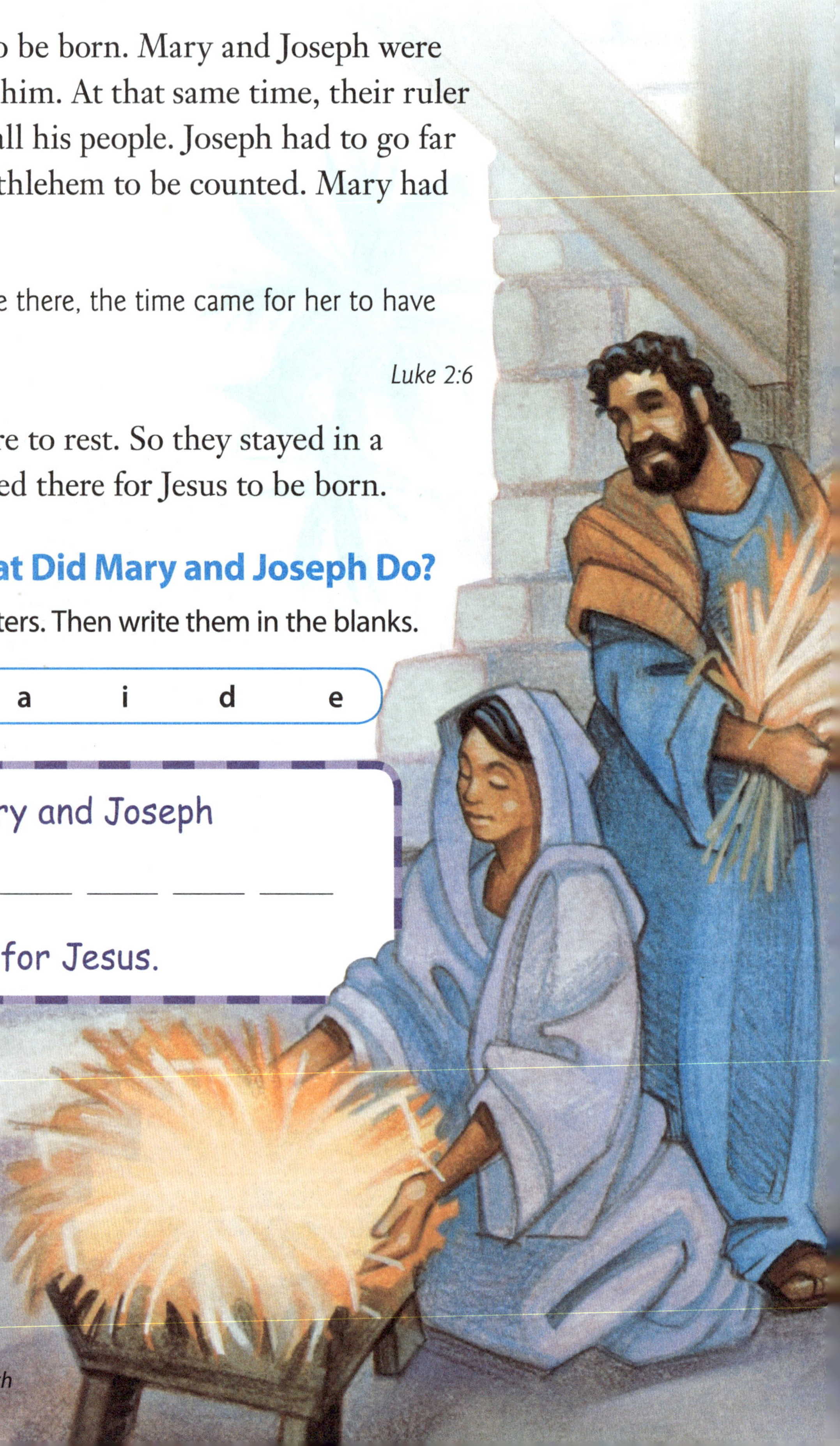

The Advent Wreath

How do you feel when you have to wait for something? It can be hard to wait. Sometimes our wait is worth it!

The Advent wreath reminds us we are waiting to celebrate the birth of Jesus. It reminds us Jesus is coming.

The Advent wreath has four candles. Usually the wreath has three violet candles and one rose candle. We light one more candle each week. Each lit candle reminds us that Christmas is getting closer.

ACTIVITY: Celebrate Advent

Write how you will celebrate Advent.

I will ______________________________

____

____

______________________________________.

Prayer Service

Leader: Jesus is the light of the world.
A reading from the Book of Isaiah.

Arise! Shine, for your light has come,
the glory of the LORD has dawned upon you.
Though darkness covers the earth,
and thick clouds, the peoples,
Upon you the LORD will dawn,
and over you his glory will be seen.

Isaiah 60:1–2

The Word of the Lord.

All: Thanks be to God.

Leader: Dear God, help us be children of the light. Guide us as we prepare for the coming of Jesus.

All: Come, Lord Jesus.

Christmas

When Jesus was born, shepherds were in the fields watching their sheep. Angels came to the shepherds. The angels told them that Jesus was born. Then the angels said,

> "Glory to God in the highest
> and on earth peace to those on whom his
> favor rests."
>
> *Luke 2:14*

During the Christmas season, we celebrate Jesus' birth. We praise God the Father for sending his Son, Jesus, to us.

Prayer

Thank you, God the Father, for sending us your Son, Jesus.

In Search of Jesus

When the angels went away from them to heaven, the shepherds said to one another, "Let us go, then, to Bethlehem to see this thing that has taken place, which the Lord has made known to us."

Luke 2:15

The shepherds were very happy. They went to find Jesus.

God the Father's Gift to Everyone

God the Father sent his Son, Jesus, to Mary and Joseph. The Father sent Jesus to the shepherds. The Father sent Jesus to us. Jesus is a gift to all of us.

Good News

The angels told the shepherds the Good News. Jesus, the Prince of Peace, was born. We can be like Jesus. We can help one another live in peace. We can obey our parents. We can be nice to our brothers and sisters.

ACTIVITY: Search for Jesus

Help the shepherds find Jesus. Draw a line along the path.

Prayer Service

Leader: Blessed be God.

All: Now and forever.

Leader: We celebrate the Good News of Jesus' birth. Let us welcome him into our lives. Let us live in peace together.

A reading from the Book of Isaiah.

For a child is born to us, a son is given to us;
upon his shoulder dominion rests.
They call him Wonder-Counselor, God-Hero,
Father-Forever, Prince of Peace.
His dominion is vast
and forever peaceful.

Isaiah 9:5–6

The Word of the Lord.

All: Thanks be to God.

Lent

Lent is the season before Easter. Lent is an important time of year. It is a time when we remember our Baptism through which we are renewed and turn away from sin. We also prepare for Easter, when we celebrate that Jesus rose from the dead.

Prayer

Jesus, my guide, help me do good things this Lent. I want to stay close to God the Father.

Grow with God

The tree below grows near a stream. The tree is healthy. The water from the stream nourishes it. The water helps it grow strong.

We are like a healthy tree. God is like our stream. When we are close to God, we grow stronger and happier.

He is like a tree
   planted near streams of water,
   that yields its fruit in season;
Its leaves never wither;
   whatever he does prospers.

Psalm 1:3

An Important Time

The first day of Lent is called Ash Wednesday. A priest, a deacon, or a lay minister places ashes on our forehead. The ashes remind us that Lent is a time to think about God's love for us.

During Lent we do many good deeds. We are more like Jesus. We grow closer to God the Father.

ACTIVITY: Good Deeds

What good deeds will you do during Lent? Write one good deed on each leaf.

Prayer Service

Leader: Let us begin our prayer with the Sign of the Cross.

All: In the name of the Father
and of the Son
and of the Holy Spirit. Amen.

Leader: We offer God our good deeds in this time of Lent. Let us pray that they will help us grow closer to God.

A reading from the holy Gospel according to John.

"I am the vine, you are the branches. Whoever remains in me and I in him will bear much fruit."

John 15:5

The Gospel of the Lord.

All: Praise to you, Lord Jesus Christ.

Holy Week

Holy Week begins on Palm Sunday and ends on Holy Saturday. Holy Week is the last week of the 40 days of Lent. During this sacred time, we remember Jesus' life. We remember his breaking of bread at the Last Supper. We remember his suffering and Death on the Cross.

Holy Week is a time for us to think about how much Jesus loves us. It is a time for us to think about how Jesus lived. Jesus taught his friends to love others. How do you show others your love?

Prayer

Jesus, my teacher, help me show my love for others. I want to be like you.

Jesus Teaches His Friends

Jesus loved his friends very much. He wanted them to know this. Jesus decided to show them. He washed his friends' feet. Then Jesus said,

> "You call me 'teacher' and 'master,' and rightly so, for indeed I am. If I, therefore, the master and teacher, have washed your feet, you ought to wash one another's feet. I have given you a model to follow, so that as I have done for you, you should also do."
>
> *John 13:13–15*

Love One Another

Jesus showed his friends how to love others. He wanted them to do as he did. Jesus wants us to follow his example too. When we help others, we are being like Jesus.

You can follow in Jesus' footsteps. You can show others your love.

ACTIVITY: Be Like Jesus

Mark the ways you can be more like Jesus.

- ☐ Be nice to others.
- ☐ Love my family.
- ☐ Feed hungry people.
- ☐ Argue with my friend.
- ☐ Pray to God the Father.
- ☐ Forgive someone who hurt me.

Prayer Service

Leader: Jesus was sad to leave his friends. Before he left, he gave them a message.

A reading from the holy Gospel according to John.

"My children, I will be with you only a little while longer. You will look for me, and as I told the Jews, 'Where I go you cannot come,' so now I say it to you. I give you a new commandment: love one another. As I have loved you, so you also should love one another. This is how all will know that you are my disciples, if you have love for one another."

John 13:33–35

The Gospel of the Lord.

All: Praise to you, Lord Jesus Christ.

Leader: Let us always remember to walk in the footsteps of Jesus.

All: In the name of the Father
and of the Son
and of the Holy Spirit. Amen.

Easter

Easter is a happy time. We celebrate Jesus Christ's rising from the dead. His Resurrection fills us with joy.

Prayer

Jesus, my friend, help me follow you. I want to be with you always.

Looking for Jesus

Three days after Jesus died, two women went to his tomb. They saw that the stone was rolled back. The tomb was empty! Then two angels came. The angels said,

> "He is not here, but he has been raised."
>
> *Luke 24:6*

The women were filled with joy. Jesus Christ was alive! The women ran to tell their friends.

Jesus Appeared to Many

On their way the women saw Jesus. Many more people saw him too. After Jesus saw his friends, it was time for him to return to his Father. Jesus ascended into heaven. We celebrate this feast on Ascension Thursday, 40 days after the Resurrection.

The Lord's Day

Why is Sunday important? It is the day we celebrate Jesus' Resurrection. It is the Lord's Day. We celebrate by going to Mass.

ACTIVITY: The Easter Story

Put the events in order. Write 1, 2, 3, or 4 in each circle.

The women tell their friends that Jesus is alive.

The women visit the tomb.

The tomb is empty.

The women see angels.

Prayer Service

Leader: May the grace of Jesus Christ be with us all, now and forever.

All: Amen.

Leader: Jesus died and rose from the dead. He gave us new life. On Sundays we remember Jesus Christ's Resurrection.

Group A: *This is the day the Lord has made;*

Group B: *let us rejoice in it and be glad.*

Psalm 118:24

All: Alleluia! Alleluia! Alleluia!

Pentecost

After Jesus rose from the dead, he went to heaven. Then the Holy Spirit came to Jesus' friends. They were full of joy. We call this joyful time Pentecost.

Prayer

Dear Holy Spirit, help me tell others about Jesus, our Lord and Savior.

Sharing Jesus

Philip was one of Jesus' Apostles. One day, Philip was walking to another city. On the road he met a man riding in a chariot. The man was reading about God. Philip said,

> "Do you understand what you are reading?" He replied, "How can I, unless someone instructs me?" So he invited Philip to get in and sit with him.
>
> *Acts of the Apostles 8:30–31*

The Holy Spirit was in Philip's heart. Philip told the man about Jesus. The man was very happy.

He and Philip rode along the road. Soon they came to some water. The man asked Philip to baptize him. They went into the water, and Philip baptized him. The man became part of God's family.

The Holy Spirit Is with Us

The Holy Spirit was with Philip. The Holy Spirit is with us too. We can celebrate Pentecost every day. We can help others know Jesus. We can do this by telling them about Jesus. The Holy Spirit will help us.

ACTIVITY: Do a Good Deed

Show that the Holy Spirit is with you. Write your name on the line. What good deed do you want the Holy Spirit to help you do today? Write it in the dove. Then color the dove.

The Holy Spirit is with

______________________________.

Prayer Service

Leader: Jesus wants us to share what we know about him. Let us listen to what he told his followers.

A reading from Acts of the Apostles.

"But you will receive power when the holy Spirit comes upon you, and you will be my witnesses in Jerusalem, throughout Judea and Samaria, and to the ends of the earth."

Acts of the Apostles 1:8

The Word of the Lord.

All: Thanks be to God.

All Saints Day

On All Saints Day, we think of all the people in heaven. They are with God. They are part of the Church. They are saints. Here are some saints we know about.

Saint Kateri Tekakwitha

Saint Francis of Assisi

Saint Ignatius

Saint Joseph

Saint Thérèse of the Child Jesus

Saint Martin de Porres

Prayer

Dear God, help me be like the saints. I want to love you as they did.

A Day for Saints

Think about your birthday. It is a day all for you. It is a day when people show how much they love you.

Saints have a day too. We call it All Saints Day. On this day we show the saints our love. How? We think about them and how they lived as true friends of God. We ask them to pray for us.

> Help us with prayer, so that thanks may be given by many on our behalf for the gift granted us through the prayers of many.
>
> *2 Corinthians 1:11*

Saints Pray for Us

Saints are holy people who have died as true friends of God. We ask the saints for their help. We ask them to talk to God for us. The saints ask God to watch over us. The saints ask God to care for us.

Saint Martin de Porres

Children of God

Our Father loves us very much. We are called the children of God. One day we will see our Father. People in heaven are children of God. They see our Father now. They are saints.

ACTIVITY: Saint Prayer Cards

Whom do you know in heaven? Ask them to pray for you. Write the name of a saint on each card. Ask the saint to help you do or be something.

Dear ______________________________,

pray for me. Help me ______________________________

____

____.

Dear ______________________________,

pray for me. Help me ______________________________

____

____.

Prayer Service

Leader: Let us pray to God and thank him for our friends the saints.

All: We praise you, we bless you, we thank you.

Group A: Let us give glory to God.

Group B: Let us praise God's name.

All: Glory be to the Father
and to the Son
and to the Holy Spirit,
as it was in the beginning
is now, and ever shall be
world without end. Amen.

Prayers and Practices of Our Faith

Knowing and Praying Our Faith

The Bible and You

God the Father speaks to us in many ways. One way is through the Bible. The Bible is the Word of God. It tells about God's promise to care for us. We learn about God the Father and Jesus' love for us. We learn how we can share God's love with others.

At Mass we hear stories from the Bible. The writings are called Scriptures. These writings are sacred, or holy.

The Bible is many books in one book. The books are separated into two parts.

One part is the Old Testament. It has 46 books in it. Stories in the Old Testament happened before Jesus was born. These stories tell how people believed in God. They believed in his promise to care for them.

The other part is the New Testament. It has 27 books in it. The New Testament tells us what Jesus said and did. Stories about Jesus' life are in the four Gospels. The word *gospel* comes from a Greek word meaning "good news." After we hear a reading from one of the four Gospels, we reply "Praise to you, Lord Jesus Christ."

We can read the Bible on our own. A Bible passage is listed like this: Genesis 2:1–3. It stands for the Book of Genesis, chapter 2, verses 1 through 3.

Prayer and How We Pray

Prayer is talking to God from your heart. Prayer is also listening closely to God speaking to you in your heart.

God is everywhere. We can pray to God at any time. We can pray to God in any place. God hears all our prayers.

We can learn prayers. We can pray in our own words too. We can listen to what God tells us. Sometimes we can just be quiet and enjoy being with God.

We pray to God from our heart. We pray often and in different ways. We can praise God. We can ask God for what we need. We can thank him. We can pray for ourselves and for others.

Sometimes we pray alone. Sometimes we pray with others. Sometimes we pray silently. Sometimes we pray aloud.

Prayers to Take to Heart

It is good for us to know prayers by heart. To take prayers to heart means that we learn, or memorize, the words. It also means that we understand and live the words.

Prayer

Sign of the Cross

In the name of the Father

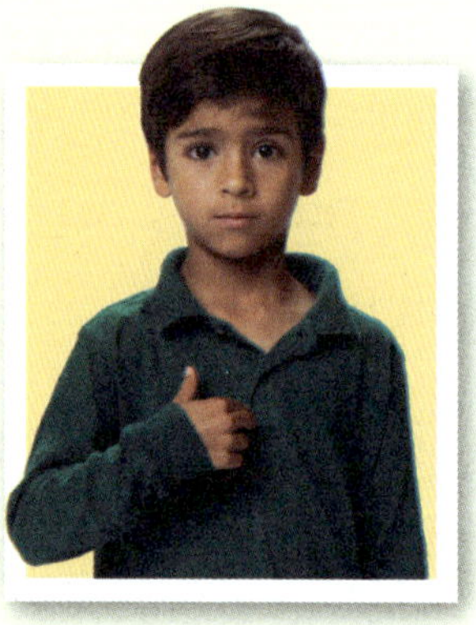

and of the Son

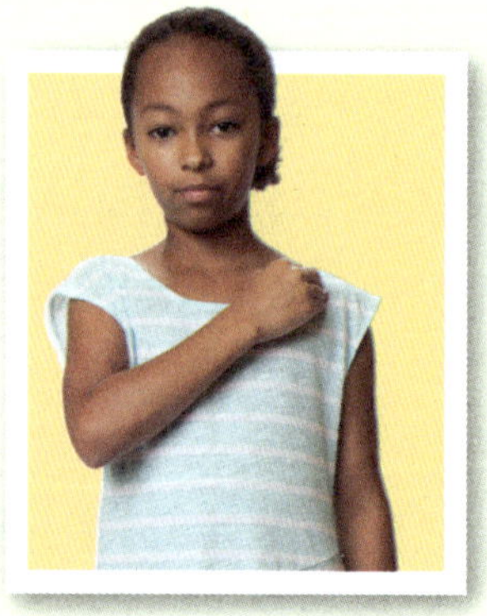

and of the Holy

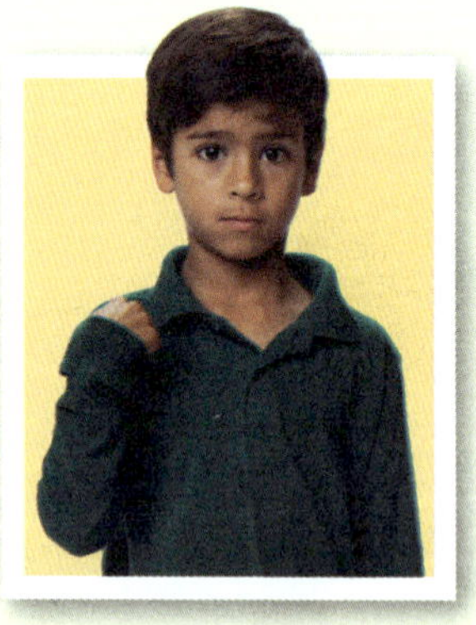

Spirit.

Amen.

Glory Be to the Father

Glory be to the Father
and to the Son
and to the Holy Spirit,
as it was in the beginning
is now, and ever shall be
world without end. Amen.

Lord's Prayer

Our Father who art in heaven,
hallowed be thy name;
thy kingdom come,
thy will be done
on earth, as it is in heaven.
Give us this day our daily bread,
and forgive us our trespasses,
as we forgive those who trespass against us;
and lead us not into temptation,
but deliver us from evil.

Hail Mary

Hail, Mary, full of grace,
the Lord is with thee.
Blessed art thou among women
and blessed is the fruit of thy womb, Jesus.
Holy Mary, Mother of God,
pray for us sinners,
now and at the hour of our death.
Amen.

Praying the Rosary

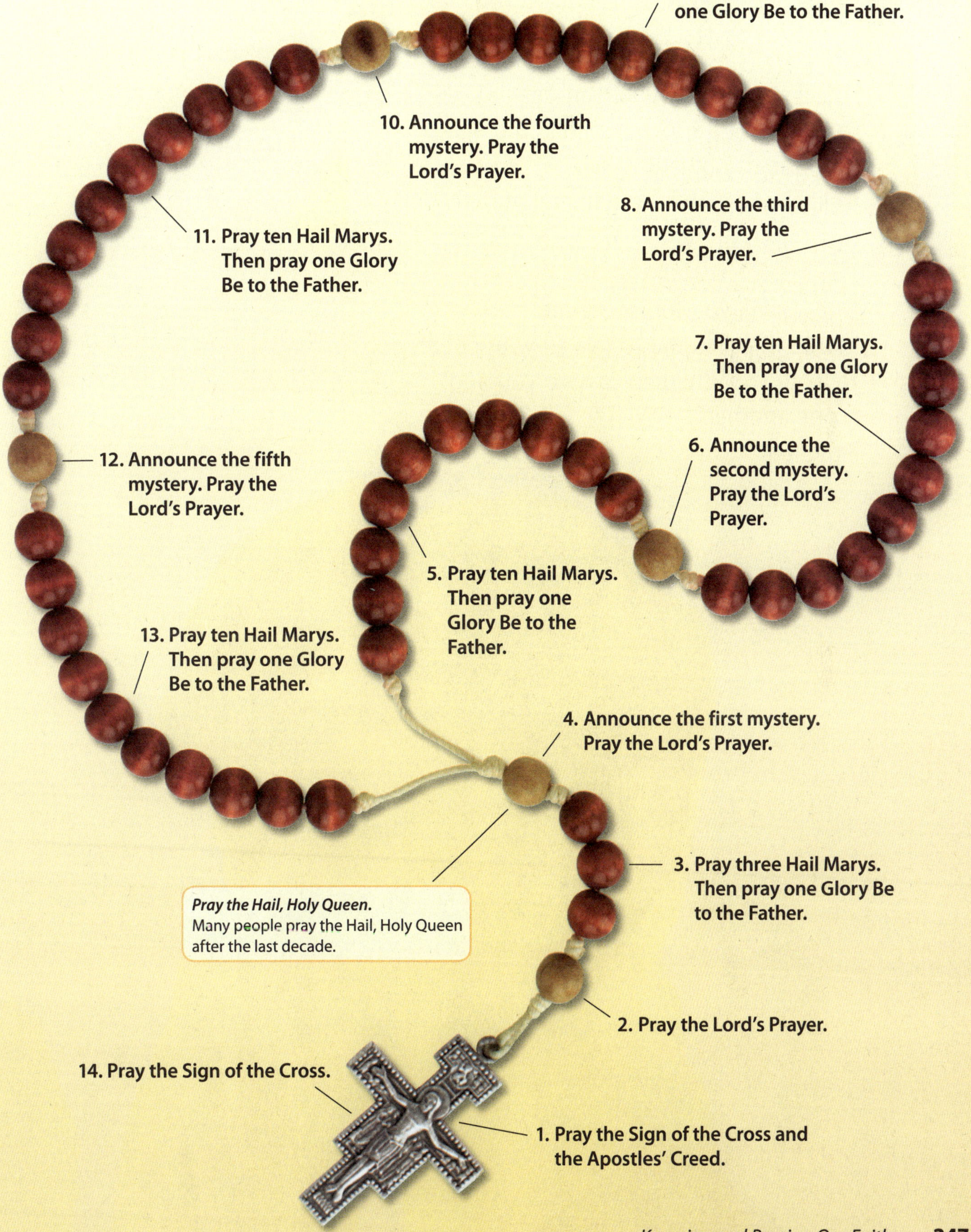

Prayer to One's Guardian Angel

Angel of God, my guardian dear,
to whom God's love commits me here,
ever this day be at my side,
to light and guard, to rule and guide. Amen.

Prayer for Vocations

God, thank you for loving me.
You have called me to live as your child.
Help all your children to love you and
one another.
Amen.

Morning Prayer

God, our Father, I offer you today all that I think
and do and say.
I offer it with what was done on earth
by Jesus Christ, your Son.
Amen.

Evening Prayer

God, our Father, this day is done.
We ask you and Jesus Christ, your Son,
that with the Spirit, our welcome guest,
you guard our sleep and bless our rest.
Amen.

Grace Before Meals

Bless us, O Lord, and these thy gifts,
which we are about to receive from
thy bounty, through Christ our Lord. Amen.

Grace After Meals

We give thee thanks, for all thy
benefits, Almighty God, who live
and reign for ever. Amen.

Celebrating Our Faith

The Seven Sacraments

A sacrament is a sign of Jesus' love. When we celebrate the sacraments, God blesses us with grace. Grace makes us strong and fills us with love.

Celebrating sacraments helps us live the way God wants us to live. Priests lead the celebration of the sacraments.

Three sacraments welcome us into the Church. They are called Sacraments of Initiation. Two sacraments heal us. They are called Sacraments of Healing. Two sacraments help us serve others. They are called Sacraments at the Service of Communion.

Baptism

Baptism is a Sacrament of Initiation. It is the first sacrament we celebrate. At Baptism a priest or deacon pours blessed water on us. We are freed from Original Sin. We become part of God's family, the Church.

Confirmation

Confirmation is a Sacrament of Initiation. At Confirmation the bishop places blessed oil on our foreheads. He prays for the Holy Spirit to make us stronger in faith.

Eucharist

Eucharist is a Sacrament of Initiation. During the Consecration at Mass, the priest blesses the wheat bread and grape wine. Jesus Christ now is present under the appearances of bread and wine. What looks like bread and wine is now the Body and Blood of Jesus Christ. We give thanks to God the Father for giving us the Body and Blood of his Son, Jesus Christ.

Penance and Reconciliation

Penance and Reconciliation is a Sacrament of Healing. We celebrate God's forgiveness. We are sorry for our sins. We tell our sins to the priest. We tell him that we are sorry. The priest gives us absolution. He tells us that God forgives us. Then the priest gives us a penance. Penance is a prayer or good deed. Doing a penance shows God that we are sorry.

Anointing of the Sick

Anointing of the Sick is a Sacrament of Healing. In this sacrament the priest blesses a person who is sick. The priest asks for God's grace to be with the person who is sick. Jesus brings his strength, peace, and courage to the person who is suffering.

Holy Orders

Holy Orders is a Sacrament at the Service of Communion. Some baptized men are called to be deacons, priests, or bishops. They receive the Sacrament of Holy Orders. They do God's work as they serve the Church. They guide us and teach us about God. Priests and bishops celebrate the sacraments with us.

Matrimony

Matrimony is a Sacrament at the Service of Communion. Some men and women are called to be married. God's grace helps them love each other. They promise to be faithful to each other for life. They share God's love with their children.

Celebrating the Lord's Day

Sunday is the main day on which we celebrate the Resurrection of Jesus. Sunday is the Lord's Day. We gather for Mass, and we rest from work. People all over the world gather at God's eucharistic table as brothers and sisters.

The Order of Mass

The Mass is the most important sacramental celebration of the Church. The Mass always follows a set order.

Introductory Rites

During the Introductory Rites, we prepare to celebrate the Eucharist.

Entrance Procession

We gather as a community and praise God in song.

1

Greeting (Sign of the Cross)

We pray the Sign of the Cross. The priest welcomes us.

2

Penitential Act (*Confiteor*)

We remember our sins and ask God for mercy.

3

Glory to God

We praise God in song.

4

Collect Prayer

We ask God to hear our prayers.

5

Liturgy of the Word

During the Liturgy of the Word, we hear God's plan of salvation.

First Reading

We listen to God's Word, usually from the Old Testament.

1

Responsorial Psalm

We respond to God's Word in song.

2

Second Reading

We listen to God's Word from the New Testament.

3

Gospel Acclamation

We sing "Alleluia!" to praise God for the Good News. During Lent we use a different acclamation to praise God for his Word.

4

Gospel

We stand and listen to the Gospel of the Lord.

5

Homily

The priest or deacon explains God's Word.

6

Profession of Faith

We proclaim our faith through the Creed.

7

Prayer of the Faithful

We pray for our needs and the needs of others.

8

Liturgy of the Eucharist

During the Liturgy of the Eucharist, we celebrate Jesus Christ's presence in the Eucharist.

Preparation of the Gifts and the Altar

We bring gifts of bread and wine to the altar.

1

Prayer over the Offerings

The priest prays that God will accept our sacrifice.

2

Eucharistic Prayer

This prayer of thanksgiving is the center and high point of the entire celebration. During this prayer the bread and wine are consecrated by the priest and through transubstantiation become the Body and Blood of Jesus Christ.

3

4

Communion Rite

We prepare to receive the Body and Blood of Jesus Christ.

The Lord's Prayer

We pray the Lord's Prayer.

5

Rite of Peace

We offer one another a sign of Christ's peace.

6

Fraction Rite

The priest breaks the consecrated host.

7

Holy Communion

We receive the Body and Blood of Jesus Christ.

8

9

Prayer After Communion

We pray that the Eucharist will strengthen us to live as Jesus did.

10

Concluding Rites

We hear announcements sometimes, but we always receive a blessing. Then we go in peace to share God's love.

People and Things I See at Mass

chasuble
deacon
priest
crucifix
cantor
altar
chalice

Living Our Faith

The Ten Commandments

Rules keep us safe. Rules help us live in peace. God gives us rules too. We call them the Ten Commandments. We can show our love for God by following the commandments.

1. I am your God; love nothing more than me.
2. Use God's name with respect.
3. Keep the Lord's Day holy.
4. Honor and obey your parents.
5. Treat all human life with respect.
6. Respect married life.
7. Respect what belongs to others.
8. Tell the truth.
9. Honor the family relationships of your neighbors and friends.
10. Be happy with what you have.

The Great Commandment

People asked Jesus, "What is the most important commandment?" Jesus said,

> "You shall love the Lord, your God, with all your heart, with all your soul, and with all your mind. This is the greatest and the first commandment. The second is like it: You shall love your neighbor as yourself."
>
> *Matthew 22:37–39*

We call this the Great Commandment.

Showing Our Love for the World

Jesus taught us to care for those in need. The Church teaches us how to do this. We practice what Jesus taught us. We make it a habit to care for others. We make it a habit to care for God's creation.

Life and Dignity

We all are made in God's image. We care for everyone as God does. We respect all people. We do things to help people. We make people more important than things in our lives.

Family and Community

Jesus wants us to be loving helpers in our families and communities.

Rights and Responsibilities

All people have a right to life. All people have a right to things they need for a good life. Jesus calls us to protect these rights for one another, for our families, and for all people.

The Poor and Vulnerable

Jesus calls us to help people who have little money and few things. We share God's creation with them. We share what we have with them. We put their needs first.

Work and Workers

The work that we do gives glory to God.

Solidarity

Since God is our Father, we treat everyone in the world as a brother or a sister. We treat everyone with respect. We care for one another. We share God's love. We make decisions for the good of everyone.

God's Creation

We show our love for God's world by taking care of it. We care for God's creation so everyone can enjoy it.

Glossary

A

absolution The forgiveness of sin by God. In the Sacrament of Penance and Reconciliation, we say that we are sorry for our sins. Then the priest offers us God's absolution.

Advent A time of joyful preparation for the celebration of Jesus' birth, beginning four Sundays before Christmas

All Saints Day November 1, the day on which the Church honors all who have died and now live with God as saints in heaven. These saints include all those who have been declared saints by the Church and many others known only to God.

All Souls Day November 2, the day on which the Church remembers all who have died as friends of God. We pray that they may rest in peace.

Alleluia A joyful prayer of praise to God. It is usually sung before the Gospel Reading at Mass.

altar The table in the church on which the priest celebrates Mass. On this table, the bread and wine are offered to God and become the Body and Blood of Jesus Christ.

ambo A desk or stand from which a person reads the Word of God during Mass

Amen The last word in any prayer that we pray. *Amen* means "This is true." We pray Amen to show that we really mean the words we have just said.

angel A messenger from God

Ash Wednesday The first day of Lent. We receive ashes on our foreheads on this day to remind us to show sorrow for the choices we make that hurt our friendships with God and with others.

B

Baptism The first sacrament. Baptism makes us part of God's family, the Church.

Beatitudes The eight ways taught by Jesus, by which we can think and act as his followers

Bible A collection of writings about God's promise to care for us, especially through his Son, Jesus. The Bible is the Word of God.

bishop A man who is an ordained leader in the Church and a successor to the Apostles. Bishops teach us what God is asking of us as followers of Jesus today.

Blessed Sacrament The Eucharist that has been consecrated by the priest at Mass. It is kept in the tabernacle for adoration and for extraordinary ministers of Holy Communion to take Holy Communion to the sick.

Body and Blood of Christ The bread and wine that have been consecrated by the priest at Mass

Bread of Life A title for Jesus that tells us he is the bread, or food, for the faithful

C

catholic A word that means "all over the world." The Church is catholic because Jesus gave the Church to the whole world.

celebrant A bishop or priest who leads the people in praying the Mass

celebrate To praise or worship God in a formal way

chasuble The visible, ceremonial garment worn by the bishop or priest at Mass

Christ A title, like *Messiah,* that means "anointed one." *Christ* is the name given to Jesus after the Resurrection.

Christian The name given to people who want to live as Jesus taught us to live

Christmas December 25, the day on which we celebrate the birth of Jesus

Church The name given to the followers of Christ all over the world. When spelled with a small *c*, *church* is the name of the building in which we gather to pray to God.

commandment A rule that tells us how to live as God wants us to live

confession The act of telling our sins to a priest in the Sacrament of Penance and Reconciliation

Confirmation The sacrament that completes the grace we receive in Baptism

conscience The inner voice that helps each of us know what God wants us to do

consecration The making of a thing or person to be set aside for God's purposes through prayer. At Mass, the words of the priest are a consecration of the bread and wine. This makes them the Body and Blood of Jesus Christ.

contrition The true sadness we feel when we know that we have sinned and wish to be forgiven

creation Everything that God has made. God said that all of creation is good.

Creator God, who made everything that is

crosier The staff carried by a bishop. This staff shows that the bishop cares for us in the same way that a shepherd cares for his sheep.

D

deacon A man who is ordained to serve the Church. Deacons participate with the bishop and priests in the work of the Church.

disciple A person who knows, loves, and follows Jesus Christ and lives according to his teaching

E

Easter The celebration of the bodily raising of Jesus Christ from the dead. Easter is the most important Christian feast.

Emmanuel A name that means "God with us." It is a name given to Jesus.

eternal life Living joyfully with God in this world and in heaven after we die

Eucharist The sacrament in which we give thanks to God for giving us the Body and Blood of Jesus Christ

Evangelists The four men credited with writing the Gospels of Matthew, Mark, Luke, and John

examination of conscience The act of thinking about what we have said or done that may have hurt our friendship with God or with others.

F

faith A gift of the Holy Spirit. Faith is the trust that we place in God and his teachings.

forgiveness The act of granting pardon to people who have said that they are sorry after hurting us. God always forgives us when we say that we are sorry. We forgive others the way God forgives us.

Fruits of the Holy Spirit The ways in which we act because we are filled with the Holy Spirit. The 12 Fruits of the Holy Spirit are love, joy, peace, patience, kindness, goodness, generosity, gentleness, faithfulness, modesty, self-control, and chastity.

G

genuflect To show respect in church, especially in front of the tabernacle, by touching a knee to the floor

gestures The movements we make, such as the Sign of the Cross or bowing, to express ourselves in prayer

God The Father, Son, and Holy Spirit. God created us, saves us, and lives in us. He is the source of salvation, and he is truth and love.

godparent A witness to Baptism who helps the baptized person live as a follower of Jesus

grace The gift of a relationship with God, given to us by God without our earning it. Grace helps us live as God wants us to live.

Great Commandment Jesus' important teaching that love of God and love of neighbor must never be separated

guardian angel The angel who has been appointed to help a person grow close to God

H

heaven The life with God that is full of joy and never ends

holy A description of something or someone set aside for God's purposes

Holy Communion The reception of the Body and Blood of Jesus Christ during Mass

holy days of obligation Those days other than Sundays on which we are committed to celebrate the great things God has done for us through Jesus Christ. Six holy days of obligation are celebrated in the United States.

Holy Family The family made up of Jesus; his mother, Mary; and his foster father, Joseph

Holy Spirit The Third Person of the Trinity, who comes to us in Baptism and Confirmation and fills us with God's life and brings us God's peace

holy water Water that has been blessed and set aside for God's purposes. Holy water is used to remind us of our Baptism.

Holy Week The week that recalls and celebrates the events of Jesus' suffering, Death, and Resurrection

Homily An explanation of God's Word by a priest or deacon at Mass. The Homily deepens our understanding of the Word of God that we hear in the Scripture readings at Mass.

honor To give the respect owed to God or a person. God is given honor as our Creator and Redeemer. All people are worthy of honor as children of God.

hope The confidence that God will always be with us. We also hope and trust that he will share his joy now and help us live in a way that keeps us with him forever.

J

Jesus The Son of God, who was born of the Virgin Mary, crucified, raised from the dead, ascended into heaven, and saves us so that we can live with God forever. The name *Jesus* means "God saves."

Joseph The foster father of Jesus, who was engaged to Mary when the angel announced that Mary would have a child through the power of the Holy Spirit

K

Kingdom of God God's rule over us. We experience the Kingdom of God in part now, and we will experience it fully in heaven.

L

Last Supper The last meal that Jesus ate with his disciples on the night before he died. Every Mass is a remembrance of that last meal.

Lectionary for Mass The book from which the stories from the Bible are read at Mass

Lent The 40 days during which we prepare to renew our Baptism and celebrate the rising of Jesus from the dead at Easter. Jesus rose from the dead to save us.

Light of the World A name for God's Son, Jesus, that helps us see that he is the light that leads us to the Father

liturgical year The celebration throughout the year of the events in the lives of Jesus, Mary, and the saints. The events of the liturgical year are organized on a liturgical calendar.

liturgy The public prayer of the Church that celebrates the wonderful things God has done for us in Jesus Christ

Liturgy of the Eucharist The part of Mass in which the bread and wine are consecrated and become the Body and Blood of Jesus Christ. We receive the Body and Blood of Jesus Christ in Holy Communion.

Liturgy of the Word A main part of the Mass in which we listen to readings of God's Word from Scripture

M

Magnificat Mary's song of praise to God. She praises God for the great things he has done for her and for his plans for us through his Son, Jesus.

Mary The mother of Jesus. She is blessed and "full of grace" because God chose her to be the Mother of Jesus, the Son of God. Mary is the Mother of the Church.

Mass The most important celebration of our faith. At Mass we listen to God's Word from Scripture and receive the Body and Blood of Jesus Christ under the appearances of bread and wine.

Messiah A title that means "anointed one." *Messiah* also means "Savior."

ministry The service or work done for others in the name of the Church

miracle The unexpected healing of a person or an occasion when nature is controlled because of God's action

moral choice A choice to do what is right. We make moral choices because they help us grow closer to God.

mortal sin A choice to turn away from God by doing something that we know is seriously wrong

N

Nativity scene A picture or display that shows Jesus, Mary, and Joseph in the stable after the birth of Jesus, as described in the Gospels of Matthew and Luke

neighbor Every person other than ourselves

New Testament The part of the Bible that contains the story of Jesus and the early Church

O

obey To follow the teachings given by God or by someone who has the right to direct us

Old Testament The part of the Bible that contains the story of God's plan for salvation before the birth of Jesus

Ordinary Time The longest liturgical season of the Church year. It is divided into two periods—one after the Christmas season and one after Pentecost.

Original Sin Our human tendency to sin, which is the result of the sin of Adam and Eve. They chose to follow their own will rather than God's will.

P

parable One of the creative stories that Jesus told to show us what God wants for the world

parish A community of believers in Jesus Christ who meet regularly to worship God together and serve one another

peacemaker A person who teaches others to be respectful in their words and actions toward one another

penance An action we perform to show we are turning away from sin so that we can live as God wants us to live

Penance and Reconciliation The sacrament in which we celebrate God's forgiveness of our sins when we tell the priest that we are sorry for them

Pentecost The 50th day after Jesus was raised from the dead. On this day, the Holy Spirit was sent from heaven, and the Church began.

petition A request we make to God, asking for what we need most. We petition God through prayer.

pope The Bishop of Rome, successor of Saint Peter, and leader of the Catholic Church

praise To give glory to God because God is so good. We can praise God through our thoughts, our words, and our actions.

prayer The act of talking to God and listening to him in our hearts

priest A man who is ordained to serve the Church. Priests guide the Church and lead it in the celebration of the sacraments.

psalm A prayer of praise in the form of a song or poem

R

reconciliation The act of repairing a friendship after it has been broken by some action or lack of action. In the Sacrament of Penance and Reconciliation, we are reconciled with God, the Church, and others.

Resurrection The bodily raising of Jesus Christ from the dead on the third day after he died on the Cross

rite The tradition and ritual that we follow in celebrating each sacrament

S

sacrament One of the seven signs/rituals given to the Church by Jesus to help us encounter God. The seven sacraments are Baptism, Confirmation, the Eucharist, Penance and Reconciliation, Anointing of the Sick, Matrimony, and Holy Orders.

Sacraments at the Service of Communion The two sacraments that help us serve others. Matrimony and Holy Orders are the Sacraments at the Service of Communion.

Sacraments of Healing The two sacraments that heal our souls and bodies. There are two Sacraments of Healing: Anointing of the Sick is one, and Reconciliation is the other.

Sacraments of Initiation The three sacraments that make us full members of God's Church. Baptism, Confirmation, and the Eucharist are the Sacraments of Initiation.

Sacrifice of the Mass The offering of Jesus Christ to God the Father under the appearances of bread and wine. We remember and experience Jesus' sacrifice every time we celebrate Mass.

saint A holy person who has died as a true friend of God and now lives with God forever in heaven

Savior Jesus, the Son of God, who became man to make us friends with God again. *Jesus* means "God saves."

Scripture The holy writings in the Bible

seal of confession The duty of a priest to keep absolutely secret the sins that are confessed to him in the Sacrament of Penance and Reconciliation

Sign of Peace The part of the Mass during the Communion Rite in which we offer a gesture of Christ's peace to one another as a sign of unity

sin A choice we make that offends God and hurts our relationship with others. A sin is an offense against God.

Son of God The name given to Jesus that reveals his special relationship to God the Father

T

tabernacle The sacred box or container in which the Blessed Sacrament is kept so that Holy Communion can be taken to those who are sick

Temple The place of worship in Jerusalem that was built by King Solomon. The Jewish people believed that this was the place of God's presence. Jesus often came to pray in the Temple.

temptation A thought or feeling that can lead us to disobey God. Temptation can come either from outside us or inside us.

Ten Commandments The 10 rules that God gave to Moses. The Ten Commandments sum up God's Law of Love and show us how to live as his children.

transubstantiation The complete change of the bread and wine into the Body and Blood of Jesus Christ

trespass An act that harms others. If someone trespasses, he or she commits an offense, or a sin.

Trinity The mystery of one God existing in Three Persons: the Father, the Son, and the Holy Spirit

V

venial sin A choice we make that weakens our relationship with God or with other people

vestments The specific clothing that a priest or bishop wears when celebrating Mass. The colors of vestments coordinate with the colors of the liturgical year and the Church feasts.

W

Word of God The Bible, which reveals the story of God's plan to save his people

Index

R

S

T

V

W

Z

Acknowledgments

Front Matter i Marina Seoane

Unit 1 1(bd) BahadirTanriover/iStock/Getty Images; (tl) Claudine Gévry; (tr) Susan Tolonen; (c) Stockbyte/Getty Images; (bl) keeweeboy/iStock/Getty Images; (b) Nika Art/Shutterstock.com; (bg) tomograf/iStock/Getty Images. **2–3** Claudine Gévry. **3**(tr) michal812/Shutterstock.com; (c) zokru/iStock/Getty Images. **4** Thomas_EyeDesign/iStockphoto/Getty Images; (b, br) Beastfromeast/Digital Vision Vectors/Getty Images. **6**(tl) Ljupco Smokovski/Shutterstock.com; (tc) AVTG/iStock/Getty Images; (tr) BananaStock/Getty Images; (bl) Hung_Chung_Chih/iStock/Getty Images; (bc) JPecha/E+/Getty Images; (br) a40757/iStock/Getty Images. **7**(t) Jobalou/iStock/Getty Images; (b) BraunS/E+/Getty Images. **8**(b) Loyola Press Photography. **9**(t) keeweeboy/iStock/Getty Images; (b) Warling Studios. **10**(t) thawats/iStock/Getty Images; (c) Kathryn Seckman Kirsch; (b) karandaev/iStock/Getty Images. **11** Jupiterimages/Stockbyte/Getty Images. **12**(t) AlekseySagitov/iStock/Getty Images; (b) bokan76/iStock/Getty Images; (bl) OttoKrause/iStock/Getty Images; (br) mimibubu/Shutterstock.com. **14**(t) Warling Studios; (c) FatCamera/E+/Getty Images; (b) Warling Studios; (bg) estherhavensphotography/iStock/Getty Images. **15** beakraus/iStock/Getty Images. **17** AJ_Watt/iStock/Getty Images. **18**(t) ZoneCreative/iStock/Getty Images; (c) Nan Brooks; (b) Rasica/iStock/Getty Images. **19**(t) andresr/E+/Getty Images; (c) Warling Studios; (br) Thomas_EyeDesign/E+/Getty Images. **20**(tl) FatCamera/E+/Getty Images; (tr) jarenwicklund/iStock/Getty Images; (c) Liderina/iStock/Getty Images; (b) Spotmatik/iStock/Getty Images; (b) Claudine Gévry. **22**(t) TheDman/iStock/Getty Images; (c) Kathryn Seckman Kirsch/Loyola Press; (b) ISMODE/iStock/Getty Images. **23** aldomurillo/E+/Getty Images. **24** Yoshi Miyake. **25**(t) _Vilor/iStock/Getty Images; (b) ArtMarie/iStock/Getty Images. **26**(t) filipfoto/iStock/Getty Images; (c) jakkapan21/iStock/Getty Images; (b) Ruslanshug/iStock/Getty Images. **27** FatCamera/iStock/Getty Images. **28**(t) GeorgeRudy/iStock/Getty Images; (b) FatCamera/E+/Getty Images. **29**(t) mammuth/E+/Getty Images; (br) AnnaRassadnikova/iStock/Getty Images; (b) Vik_Y/iStock/Getty Images. **30** David LaFleur. **31** David LaFleur. **32**(l) KathrynSK/DigitalVision Vectors/Getty Images. **33**(t) maljuk/Shutterstock.com; (b) baona/E+/Getty Images. **34**(t) Elena Shutova/iStock/Getty Images; (c) Olwyn Whelan; (b) Monkey Business Images/Shutterstock.com. **35** Susan Tolonen. **36**(t) Kunst Bilder/Shutterstock.com; (b) bowdenimages/iStock/Getty Images. **37**(t) Private Collection/Photo © The Maas Gallery, London/Bridgeman Images; (c) Color Brush/Shutterstock.com; (b) Nika Art/Shutterstock.com. **38**(t) madisonwi/iStock/Getty Images; (c) NiroDesign/iStock/Getty Images; (b) Stockbyte/Getty Images. **39**(t) Warling Studios; Avalon_Studio/iStock/Getty Images; eyewave/iStock/Getty Images; Avalon_Studio/iStock/Getty Images; (b) SonerCdem/iStock/Getty Images. **40**(t, c) KathrynSK/DigitalVision Vectors/Getty Images. **41**(t) Baby2M/Shutterstock.com; (c) Hyrma/iStock/Getty Images; (b) Claudine Gévry. **42**(t) Claudine Gévry; (b) JohnnyGreig/E+/Getty Images.

Unit 2 43(tl) Claudine Gévry; (tr) Videowok_art/iStock/Getty Images; (ct) AnYudina/iStock/Getty Images; (cb) The Crosiers/Gene Plaisted, OSC; (bl) Warling Studios; (b) Smileus/iStock/Getty Images. **44** Claudine Gévry. **45** Antonel/iStock/Getty Images. **46** Muralinath/iStock/Getty Images. **47**(t) The Holy Family at Nativity, 2007 (acrylic on canvas), James, Laura (Contemporary Artist)/Private Collection/Bridgeman Images; (b) Claudine Gévry. **48**(t) stereohype/iStock/Getty Images; (c) Kathryn Seckman Kirsch; (b) David LaFleur. **49**(tl) Jupiterimages/Stockbyte/Getty Images; (tc) Wavebreakmedia Ltd/Wavebreak Media/Getty Images; (tr) kiankhoon/iStock/Getty Images; (bl) Jupiterimages/Polka Dot/Getty Images; (br) bowdenimages/iStock/Getty Images. **50** Yoshi Miyake. **51**(t) Videowok_art/iStock/Getty Images Plus/Getty Images; (b) kali9/E+/Getty Images. **52**(t) chaluk/iStock/Getty Images; (c) Nan Brooks; (b) Nottomanv1/iStock/Getty Images. **53** andresr/E+/Getty Images. **54**(t) mammuth/E+/Getty Images; (b) Geber86/E+/Getty Images. **55**(t) Great crowds followed Jesus as he preached the Good News, 2004 (w/c on paper), Wang, Elizabeth (1942–2016)/Private Collection/© Radiant Light/Bridgeman Images; (b) AlexGreenArt/Shutterstock.com. **56** David LaFleur. **58**(t) Tatyana Okhitina/Shutterstock.com; (b) Nova Development Art Explosion. **59** ozgurdonmaz/iStock/Getty Images. **60**(t) retrorocket/iStock/Getty Images; (cl) AlexD75/E+/Getty Images; (cr) Comstock Images/Stockbyte/Getty Images; (bl) Jupiterimages/Goodshoot RF/Getty Images; (br) Warling Studios. **61**(t) The Crosiers/Gene Plaisted, OSC; (b) beastfromeast/iStock/Getty Images. **62**(t) anna1311/iStock/Getty Images; (b) fotostorm/E+/Getty Images. **63**(t) Pater Noster—The Lord's Prayer, illustration for 'The Life of Christ', c.1886–94 (w/c & gouache on paperboard), Tissot, James Jacques Joseph (1836–1902)/Brooklyn Museum of Art, New York, USA/Bridgeman Images; (b) Undrey/Shutterstock.com. **64**(t) kali9/E+/Getty Images; (b) Alistair Berg/Digital Vision/Getty Images. **65**(t) milosluz/iStock/Getty Images; (b) romrodinka/iStock/Getty Images; (bg) zocchi2/iStock/Getty Images. **66** Yoshi Miyake. **67** mr_oji/iStock/Getty Images. **68**(tl) alashi/DigitalVision Vectors/Getty Images; (tr) benchart/Shutterstock.com; (cl) bortonia/DigitalVision Vectors/Getty Images; (cr) yelet/iStock/Getty Images; (b) SanneBerg/iStock/Getty Images. **69**(t) Warling Studios; (b) Smileus/iStock/Getty Images. **70**(t) o-che/iStock/Getty Images; (c) Kathryn Seckman Kirsch; (b) edgardr/iStock/Getty Images. **71**(t) The Women at the Sepulchre, illustration from 'Women of the Bible', published by The Religious Tract Society, 1927 (colour litho), Copping, Harold (1863 –1932) / Private Collection / Bridgeman Images; (c) AnYudina/iStock/Getty Images. **72** David LaFleur. **73** David LaFleur. **74** AnnaRassadnikova/iStock/Getty Images. **75** Monkey Business Images/Monkey Business/Getty Images. **76**(t) Olwyn Whelan; (b) egal/iStock/Getty Images. **77**(b) sedmak/iStock/Getty Images. **78**(t) digitalskillet/iStock/Getty Images; (c) goir/iStock/Getty Images; (b) bowdenimages/iStock/Getty Images. **79**(t) St. David's City, 2005 (w/c on paper), Todd, Tony (Contemporary Artist) / Private Collection / Bridgeman Images; (b) Claudine Gévry. **80**(t) Warling Studios; (b) Kathryn Seckman Kirsch. **81** Kathryn Seckman Kirsch. **83**(t) Jupiterimages/Stockbyte/Getty Images; (bl) pkline/iStock/Getty Images; (br) Kathryn Seckman Kirsch. **84**(t) vaeenma/iStock/Getty Images; (b) Warling Studios.

Unit 3 85(t) Claudine Gévry; (bd) lilly3/iStock/Getty Images; (t) Dado Photos/Shutterstock.com; (c, b) Claudine Gévry; (bl) Digital Vision./Photodisc/Getty Images. **86** Claudine Gévry. **87** The Crosiers/Gene Plaisted, OSC. **88**(t) Topalov/iStock/Getty Images; (b) Kathryn Seckman Kirsch. **89**(t) The Crosiers/Gene Plaisted, OSC; (b) Olga_Bonitas/iStock/Getty Images. **90**(l) Noah Seelam/Stringer/AFP/Getty Images; (rt) ROLEX DELA PENA/EPA-EFE/Shutterstock.com; (rc) shakzu/iStock/Getty Images; (rb) Hector Retamal/AFP/Getty Images. **91** LanaN/Shutterstock.com. **92** David LaFleur. **93**(t) chengyuzheng/iStock/Getty Images; (c) ILLYCH/iStock/Getty Images; (b) Lopolo/Shutterstock.com. **94**(t) littleclie/iStock/Getty Images; (b) Kathryn Seckman Kirsch. **95**(t) Warling Studios; (b) Kathryn Seckman Kirsch. **96**(t) SpeedKingz/Shutterstock.com; (b) Bill Wittman. **97**(t) The Crosiers/Gene Plaisted, OSC; (b) 4clover/Shutterstock.com. **98**(l) Bill Wittman; (r) and2DesignInc/DigitalVision Vectors/Getty Images. **99**(t) happyfoto/E+/Getty Images; (l) FrankyDeMeyer/Vetta/Getty Images; (r) imagenavi/Getty Images. **100**(br) KathrynSK/DigitalVision Vectors/Getty Images. **101** DenKuvaiev/iStock/Getty Images. **102** Olwyn Whelan. **103**(t) monkeybusinessimages/iStock/Getty Images; (b) Kathryn Seckman Kirsch. **104**(t) Claudine Gévry; (b) Digital Vision/Photodisc/Getty Images. **105**(t) Private Collection/© Look and Learn/Bridgeman Images; (b) beastfromeast/iStock/Getty Images. **106** David LaFleur. **107**(t) David LaFleur; (c) Phil Martin Photography; (bl) Phil Martin Photography; (br) Warling Studios. **109** ozgurdonmaz/iStockphoto/Getty Images. **110**(t) anatols/iStock/Getty Images; (b) tuulijumala/iStock/Getty Images. **111**(t) Purestock/Getty Images; (b) Rawpixel Ltd/iStockphoto/Getty Images. **112** Steve Debenport/E+/Getty Images. **113**(t) Laura Michell; (b) Claudine Gévry. **114**(t) Liliboas/E+/Getty Images; (tr) C Squared Studios/Photodisc/Getty Images; (b) Blend Images Photography/Veer. **115** Jupiterimages/liquidlibrary/Getty Images. **116** Yoshi Miyake. **117**(t) AgnusImages.com; (b) real444/E+/Getty Images. **118**(t) Olwyn Whelan; (b) Kathryn Seckman Kirsch. **119** yongsuk son/iStockphoto/Getty Images. **120**(t) dianazh/iStock/Getty Images; (b) Warling Studios. **121** The Crosiers/Gene Plaisted, OSC; (b) anamad/iStock/Getty Images. **122**(t) iLexx/iStock/Getty Image; (c) AgnusImages.com; (b) iLexx/iStock/Getty Images. **123** Kathryn Seckman Kirsch. **124** Big_Ryan/DigitalVision Vectors/Getty Images. **125**(t) Dado Photos/Shutterstock.com; (b) Claudine Gévry. **126**(t) Claudine Gévry; (b) Bill Wittman.

Unit 4 127(bd) April30/iStock/Getty Images; (tl) Claudine Gévry; (tr) Claudine Gévry; (ct) Jupiterimages/Stockbyte/Getty Images; (cb) Warling Studios; (b) saemilee/DigitalVision Vectors/Getty Images. **128** Claudine Gévry. **129** 5second/iStock/Getty Images. **130** Kathryn Seckman Kirsch. **131**(t) The First Shall Be the Last, illustration for 'The Life of Christ', c.1886–94 (w/c & gouache on paperboard), Tissot, James Jacques Joseph (1836–1902)/Brooklyn Museum of Art, New York, USA/Bridgeman Images; (c) Color_Brush/iStock/Getty Images; (b) NK08gerd/iStock/Getty Images. **132**(t) stereohype/E+/Getty Images; (bl) AgnusImages.com; (bc) Warling Studios; (br) ASphotowed/iStock/Getty Images. **133** Bill Wittman. **134** Yoshi Miyake. **135** moodboard/Getty Images. **136**(t) The Crosiers/Gene Plaisted, OSC; (c) goir/iStock/Getty Images; (b) ClaudioVentrella/iStock/Getty Images. **137** Kathryn Seckman Kirsch. **138** Jeff Greenough/Blend Images/Getty Images. **139**(t) Renata Sedmakova/Shutterstock.com; (b) SovaPictures_of_ASV/iStock/Getty Images. **140**(t) Claudine Gévry; (bg) iadamson/iStock/Getty Images; (bl) Phil Martin Photography; (br) Warling Studios. **141** Warling Studios. **142**(t) David LaFleur; (b) Yoshi Miyake. **143**(t) art nick/Shutterstock.com; (b) Warling Studios. **144**(t) marekuliasz/Shutterstock.com; (l) Warling Studios; (rt) Kenny10/iStock/Getty Images; (rb) azndc/iStock/Getty Images; (bg) ilolab/Shutterstock.com. **145** Kathryn Seckman Kirsch. **146**(t) Warling Studios; (b) Digital Vision./Photodisc/Getty Images. **147**(t) The Crosiers/Gene Plaisted, OSC; (b) Svetlana Mikhalevich/Shutterstock.com. **148** David LaFleur. **149**(t) Claudine Gévry; (b) Warling Studios. **151** monkeybusinessimages/iStock/Getty Images. **152**(t) Avalon_Studio/E+/Getty Images; (c) Warling Studios; (b) Kathryn Seckman Kirsch. **153**(t) Warling Studios; (b) sedmak/iStock/Getty Images. **154**(t) Laura Michell; (b) Lightwavemedia/Getty Images. **155**(t) Evening Prayer, Burgess, John-Bagnold (1830–97)/Private Collection/Photo © Gavin Graham Gallery, London, UK/Bridgeman Images; (b) saemilee/DigitalVision Vectors/Getty Images. **156** David LaFleur. **157**(t) Aleks Melnik/Shutterstock.com; (b) DenKuvaiev/iStockphoto/Getty Images. **158** Yoshi Miyake. **159** BravissimoS/iStock/Getty Images. **160**(t) Jupiterimages/liquidlibrary/Getty Images; (c) EVAfotografie/iStock/Getty Images; (b) Lukiyanova Natalia frenta/Shutterstock.com. **161**(t) lenta/iStock/Getty Images; (b) andy_Q/iStock/Getty Images. **162**(t) The Crosiers/Gene Plaisted, OSC; (b) aldomurillo/E+/Getty Images. **163**(t) Jesus being led into the wilderness to be tempted by the devil, Hole, William Brassey (1846–1917)/Private Collection/© Look and Learn/Bridgeman Images; (b) llexImage/Vetta/Getty Images. **164**(t) Jupiterimages/Stockbyte/Getty Images; (b) Warling Studios. **165**(tl) Phil Martin Photography; (b) studio2013/Shutterstock.com. **166** Tony Rothberg. **167**(t) digitalskillet/Shutterstock.com; (b) MyImages_Micha/iStock/Getty Images. **168**(t) Warling Studios; (b) Ridofranz/iStock/Getty Images.

Unit 5 169(bd) Pierrot46/iStockphoto/Getty Images; (tl) Claudine Gévry; (tc) O-che/iStockphoto.com; (c) Laurence Dutton/The Image Bank/Getty Images; (cb) Jupiterimages/Polka Dot/Getty Images; (bl) monkeybusinessimages/iStock/Getty Images; (br) MarinaMariya/iStock/Getty Images. **170** Claudine Gévry. **171** Ars Jesuitica art collection, courtesy of The Jesuits of Missouri Province. **172** matka_Wariatka/Shutterstock.com. **173**(t) kirilart/iStock/Getty Images Plus/Getty Images; (b) Claudine Gévry. **174**(t) Jupiterimages/Polka Dot/Getty Images; (c) Wealan Pollard/OJO Images/Getty Images; (b) SW Productions/Photodisc/Getty Images. **175** bennymarty/iStock/Getty Images. **177** Sasiistock/iStock/Getty Images. **178**(t) Tomacco/iStock/Getty Images; (c) Kathryn Seckman Kirsch; (b) Kathryn Seckman Kirsch. **179** Christina Balit. **180**(t) Pinon Road/Shutterstock.com; (b) AndreasReh/iStockphoto/Getty Images. **181**(t) The Crosiers/Gene Plaisted, OSC; (b) MarinaMariya/iStock/Getty Images. **182** eurobanks/iStock/Getty Images. **183** eurobanks/iStock/Getty Images. **184** danbailey/DigitalVision Vectors/Getty Images. **185** ozgurdonmaz/iStock/Getty Images. **186** David LaFleur. **187**(t) jaroszpilewski/iStock/Getty Images; (c) shironosov/iStock/Getty Images; (b) MerggyR/iStock/Getty Images. **188**(t) Madhourse/iStock/Getty Images; (b) monkeybusinessimages/iStock/Getty Images. **189**(t) JulieLonneman; (c) Anna_Guz/iStock/Getty Images; (b) Anna_Guz/iStock/Getty Images. **190** David LaFleur. **191**(t) Laurence Dutton/The Image Bank/Getty Images; (ct) milanvirijevic/E+/Getty Images; (cb) Dean Mitchell/iStock/Getty Images; (b) FatCamera/E+/Getty Images. **192**(t) Olwyn Whelan. (b) Olwyn Whelan. **193** FatCamera/E+/Getty Images. **194**(t) digitalskillet/iStock/Getty Images; (c) Andersen Ross/Blend Images/Getty Images; (bl) Mike Kemp/Blend Images/Getty Images; (br) Jon Feingersh/Blend Images/Getty Images. **195** lasalus/iStock/Getty Images. **196**(t) The Crosiers/Gene Plaisted, OSC; (b) skynesher/Vetta/Getty Images. **197**(t) God created the earth and continues to care for it (w/c on paper), Wang, Elizabeth (1942–2016)/Private Collection/© Radiant Light/Bridgeman Images; (b) MerggyR/iStock/Getty Images. **198**(bg) krisstina/iStockphoto.com; (t) Ryan McVay/Digital Vision/Getty Images; (b) tirc83/iStock/Getty Images; (br) bo1982/iStock/Getty Images. **199**(t) fivespots/Shutterstock.com; (b) MintImages/Shutterstock.com. **200** Amanda Hall. **201**(t) AmbientIdeas/iStock/Getty Images; (b) Jupiterimages/BananaStock/Getty Images. **202**(t) jacglad/iStock/Getty Images; (c) Gelpi/Shutterstock.com; (b) temniy/E+/Getty Images. **203** AGrigorjeva/iStock/Getty Images. **204**(t) GlobalP/iStock/Getty Images; (b) kali9/iStock/Getty Images. **205**(t) Marina Seone; (b) Eglelip/iStock/Getty Images. **206**(t) O-che/iStockphoto.com; (b) Kathryn Seckman Kirsch. **207**(t) Brand X Pictures/Stockbyte/Getty Images. (b) vahlakova/iStock/Getty Images. **208** Len Ebert/PC&F Inc. **209**(t) 3sbworld/iStock/Getty Images; (b) Mitar Vidakovic/Shutterstock.com. **210**(t) Claudine Gévry; (b) FangXiaNuo/E+/Getty Images.

The Year in Our Church 211 Marina Seone. **212**(t) Warling Studios; (cl) Jupiterimages/Polka Dot/Getty Images Plus/Getty Images; (cr) hohl/iStock/Getty Images Plus/Getty Images; (b) Jupiterimages/Polka Dot/Getty Images Plus/Getty Images. **213** David LaFleur. **214** David LaFleur. **215**(tl) Iness/Shutterstock.com; (tr) ghoststone/iStock/Getty Image Plus/Getty Images; (bl) ghoststone/iStock/Getty Image Plus/Getty Images; ghoststone/iStock/Getty Image Plus/Getty Images; (br) Warling Studios. **216** FangXiaNuo/E+/Getty Images. **217**(t) hudiemm/E+/Getty Images; (c) wavebreakmedia/Shutterstock.com; (b) HANS-JOACHIM SCHNEIDER/Veer; (bg) Loyola Press. **218** David LaFleur. **219** Olwyn Whelan. **220**(t) OllgaP/iStock/Getty Images Plus/Getty Images; (b) Alija/E+/Getty Images. **221**(tl) ilolab/Shutterstock.com; (tr) Comstock Images/Stockbyte/Getty Images; (c) Jupiterimages/Stockbyte/Getty Images; (bl) Monkey Business Images/Shutterstock.com; (br) Jill Chen/Stocksy United. **222** Nina Klausen/iStockphoto.com. **223**(t) Warling Studios; (c) Kathryn Seckman Kirsch; (b) Nina Klausen/iStockphoto.com. **224** Elenathewise/iStock/Getty Images. **225**(tl) pukach/Getty Images; (tr) David LaFleur; (bl) iofoto/Getty Images; (br) Thomas M Perkins/Shutterstock.com. **226** David LaFleur. **227**(t) Sean Locke/iStockphoto.com; (b) Mega Pixel/Shutterstock.com. **228** DNY59/E+/Getty Images. **229**(tl) amlet/Shutterstock.com; (tr) Kathryn Seckman Kirsch; (cl) Digital Vision./Photodisc/Getty Images; (cr) Oksana Shufrych/Shuterstock.com; (c) samantha grandy/Shuterstock.com; (bl) oliveromg/Shutterstock.com; (br) SaraStock/iStock/Getty Image Plus/Getty Images; (bg) littleclie/iStock/Getty Image Plus/Getty Images. **230**(t) ilolab/Shutterstock.com; (cl) The Crosiers/Gene Plaisted, OSC; (cr) David LaFleur; (b) sahua d/Shutterstock.com. **231**(t) David LaFleur; (b) ilolab/Shutterstock.com. **232** debibishop/E+/Getty Images. **233**(t) ptaxa/iStock/Getty Images; (b) David LaFleur. **234** David LaFleur. **235** David LaFleur. **236** JTGrafix/E+/Getty Images. **237**(tl) The Crosiers/Gene Plaisted, OSC; (tc) AgnusImages.com; (tr) CarolynCroll; (bl) The Crosiers/Gene Plaisted, OSC; (bc) CarolynCroll; (br) AgnusImages.com. **238**(tl) Andersen Ross/Blend Images/Getty Images; (bl) The Crosiers/Gene Plaisted, OSC; (br) Warling Studios. **239**(tl) Anterovium/iStock/Getty Images Plus/Getty Images; (tr) Gelpi/Shutterstock.com; (b) viviyan/DigitalVision Vectors/Getty Images. **240** Warling Studios.

Prayers and Practices of Our Faith 241(t) The Crosiers/Gene Plaisted, OSC; (c) Nino Cavalier/Shutterstock.com; (b) xavierarnau/E+/Getty Images. **242** Stockbyte/Getty Images. **243**(t) Kativ/E+/Getty Images; (b) Image Source Photography/Veer. **244**(tl) Warling Studios; (b) xavierarnau/E+/Getty Images. **245** The Crosiers/Gene Plaisted, OSC. **246** David LaFleur. **247** Greg Kuepfer. **248** wavebreakmedia/Shutterstock.com. **249**(t) David LaFleur; (b) SolStock/iStock/Getty Images. **250**(t) Alessandra Cimatoribus; (b) Phil Martin Photography. **251**(t) Alessandra Cimatoribus; (c) Alessandra Cimatoribus; (bl) h2o_color/iStock/Getty Images; (br) Warling Studios. **252**(t) Warling Studios; (c) Alessandra Cimatoribus; (bl) Alessandra Cimatoribus; (br) h2o_color/iStock/Getty Images. **253**(t) Alessandra Cimatoribus; (c) Alessandra Cimatoribus; (b) W. P. Wittman Limited. **254** Warling Studios. **255** Jill Arena, Carrie Gowran, and Karen Wolcott. **256**(t) Jill Arena, Carrie Gowran, and Karen Wolcott; (b) linearcurves/DigitalVision Vectors/Getty Images. **257**(tl) Jill Arena, Carrie Gowran, and Karen Wolcott; (tc) Jill Arena, Carrie Gowran, and Karen Wolcott; (tr) Mixmike/E+/Getty Images; (cl) Jill Arena, Carrie Gowran, and Karen Wolcott; (cr) Jill Arena, Carrie Gowran, and Karen Wolcott; (b) Warling Studios. **258** Jill Arena, Carrie Gowran, and Karen Wolcott. **259** Jill Arena, Carrie Gowran, and Karen Wolcott. **260**(t) Phil Martin Photography; (b) Claudine Gévry. **261**(l) W. P. Wittman Limited; (c) Warling Studios. **262**(t) ericmichaud/E+/Getty Images; (c) annebaek/iStock/Getty Images; (b) David LaFleur. **263**(t) saemilee/DigitalVision Vectors/Getty Images; (b) fstop123/E+/Getty Images. **264**(t) Science Photo Library/Getty Images; (b) fstop123/E+/Getty Images.